GOD
HUNGER

MEDITATIONS FROM A LIFE OF LONGING

DOMINIC MUIR

RIVER
PUBLISHING

River Publishing & Media Ltd
www.river-publishing.co.uk

info@river-publishing.co.uk

Copyright © Dominic Muir 2017

978-1-908393-64-7
Cover design by www.spiffingcovers.com

DEDICATION

To the hungry and wild at heart

CONTENTS

1. INSIDE-OUT

2. GRACE, UP CLOSE AND PERSONAL

3. THE PRESSURE'S OFF

4. HUMILITY VERSUS PRIDE

5. ENTITLED?

6. HUNGER FOR GOD

7. CONTROVERSY FOR THE SAKE OF TRUTH

8. WHAT DO YOU SEE?

9. TRUE HUMILITY

10. GODLY VERSUS SELFISH AMBITION

11. CALLED TO PURPOSE

12. HOW WILL THEY HEAR?

13. THE TRUTH ABOUT GOD THE FATHER

14. GOD IS GOOD, ALL THE TIME

15. THROUGH THE DESERT

16. THE LAW OF LONGEVITY

17. SWORD PRACTICE

18. SHIFTING OUR FOCUS

19. STRANGERS

20. LOOKING IN THE RIGHT DIRECTION

21. LIVING FROM KINGDOM VALUES

22. KINGDOM VALUES 1

23. KINGDOM VALUES 2

24. KINGDOM VALUES 3

25. KINGDOM VALUES 4

26. A DEEPER SENSE OF THANKFULNESS

27. TESTING TIMES

28. SHAME – THE EXIT OF THE SON

29. SHAME – THE RETURN OF THE SON

30. SHAME – FROM HIDING TO BELONGING

31. CHANGING OUR VIEW OF REPENTANCE

32. LOSING OURSELVES

33. TRUE HOPE

34. REALITY CHECK

35. BE FILLED AND TAKE POSSESSION

36. THE SECRET OF THE FATHER'S DISCIPLINE

37. LIMITLESS GRACE

38. A MEDITATION ON LOVE

39. CHOSEN ONES

40. ALL IS GRACE

41. IDENTITY AND AUTHORITY

42. CRAZY FOR GOD

43. THE NAME

44. LOVE VERSUS FEAR

45. TRUE FEAR

46. FIRST THINGS FIRST

47. THE INHERITANCE

48. THE BEAUTY OF MEEKNESS

49. JUSTIFIED

50. THE BATTLEFIELD OF THE MIND

51. RAW FAITH

52. TRUE GREATNESS

53. LOVE OVERCOMES

54. LOVE NEVER RUNS OUT

55. LOVE DESIRES HIS PRESENCE

56. LOVE NEVER FAILS

57. LOVE LAUGHS BUT ALSO FIGHTS

58. LOVE NEVER ENDS

59. LOVE IS TRUE

60. LOVE RISES ABOVE EVERYTHING

WHAT OTHERS ARE SAYING...

God Hunger is a rich and very ripe daily offering for a lifestyle of intimacy with Jesus Christ. Dominic has beautifully revealed how to dance through life with a depth in God that secures and roots us like nothing and no one else. There is an extensive array of revelation from other writers and lovers of the Lord too in this wonderful book, along with Dominic's own personal quest for deeper intimacy with Jesus.

I have had the privilege to travel with Dominic to India and other places and have witnessed how he pursues the deeper places of God's heart without compromise. His personal longing to belong to the Almighty alone is experienced here, page after page. I have enjoyed my journey through these pages and it has shaped my heart to receive more from God, and I'm sure it will reshape it further as I revisit these meditations again. *God Hunger* is not simply a book to be read, enjoyed and placed on your bookshelf, but one to be kept by your bedside for a daily dive into the security and richness of a good Father. Each meditation is a priceless moment with the Lord. Eat and be nourished!

Rahil Patel, former Hindu Priest and author of *Found by Love*

With a mature yet childlike faith and passionate conviction, Dominic has a gift for exploring the truth and challenging us to dive into a deeper understanding of the nature and character of God. Every exploration beautifully reveals the Father's heart and His unfailing love for His children. Dominic exposes the boundaries of our religious thinking and eloquently directs us onto a path of glorious freedom.

Tiffany Buhler, David's Tent Managing Director

Dominic has put together a collection of meditations and thoughts that are powerful and comforting. The author invites us on a 60-day journey to become more passionate, and more deeply known by Jesus, through this unswervingly Gospel-centred book of reflections. His desire is that we will each go on to impact our friends, families and work colleagues as we partner with God in His mission. A very good read that challenges and refreshes at the same time.

Revd Paul Cowley MBE, Ambassador for Social Transformation, Holy Trinity Brompton and Alpha International

This is one of the best collections of daily meditations I have ever read or seen! This is not merely another religious devotional book, it is alive. Throughout this book Dominic Muir has managed to capture me by bringing back the truth of the Scriptures and the power of the Word. Many foundational issues are touched upon and its simplicity lays a solid foundation for any believer.

God Hunger answers the questions people are asking and replaces the uncertainty with the truth. There is a growing desire among many to encounter God in the supernatural, and this book not only activates that desire, it gives us the tools in order to be able to move in the power of the Spirit. Too many, however, want to move in the Spirit without the character that is necessary to do so effectively. Dominic addresses this issue. Here he has managed to show us how we can bring heaven to earth. This is a great tool for all believers, but I believe it will also act as a catalyst for the unsaved to seek encounter and relationship with God. This book holds the key to intimacy and true relationship with Jesus. *God Hunger* is a must read! May you be blessed as Dominic takes you on a journey to intimacy and relationship with Jesus Christ.

Dr Etienne Blom, Kingdom Fire Ministries

I have loved Dominic's fresh, grace-dripping collection of meditations! There is nothing better than being reminded of just how spectacular our Father is and how deeply loved by Him we truly are. With the urgent call to passionate, mobilized mission today, it can only be sustained by a generation who know their Father intimately and who are settled in His heart's affection for them. This book will certainly spark Jesus-followers to both – and the world will get to reap the fruit eternally. Thanks for putting this together Dominic!

Ryan Matthews, Senior Pastor, Glenridge Church, Durban, South Africa

Dominic Muir is a burning, shining light in our generation and I thank God for him and his ministry. He has written 60 fine meditations. He combines a profound passion for God with a deep understanding of the human heart. With deft use of a wide range of quotations we hear his own voice clearly. These are super – they will be a great help in renewing and revitalising any life with God.

Rev John Valentine, St George's Holborn, London

I've known Dom for over 8 years and he has a passionate heart to reach the world with the Gospel. *God Hunger* is going to be a real blessing to you. It is a fantastic series of daily reflections that you can read and meditate upon. I pray it creates in you some of the passion that Dominic carries. He is such a blessing to the Body of Christ.

Rev Ian McCormack (The Jellyfish Man)

In *God Hunger* you will find amazing insights into the Scriptures and how to apply them to everyday life. The truths presented here don't come from head knowledge, but from Dom's personal experiences. He actually walks this stuff out. He's learned from his mistakes and failures – that's what qualifies him to write this powerful book. He doesn't just talk about it, he actually does it. Dom is deeply devoted to doing the will of God, no matter what the cost. I know him to be a man of great passion for the things of God, very much like a modern day John Wesley. As you apply the truths presented here, you will be well on your way to living the life God intended – to becoming all He created you to be.

Gary Oates, author *Open My Eyes, Lord*

God Hunger is a fantastic collection of meditations for anyone looking to go deeper in intimacy with God. Through it Dominic Muir challenges and inspires us to feast on all the goodness that a life devoted to God has to offer.

Caleb Meakins, Director, *Shift UK*

Dominic is a dear friend with whom I have journeyed through various seasons of life. He has a huge heart for God and there is an astonishing congruence between what he believes and how he lives. This collection of meditations is an absolute treasure trove of heavy truth, eloquently expressed by a man after God's own heart.

Pete Portal, Lead Pastor, Tree of Life, Manenberg, Cape Town

Dominic gives us a well-rounded devotional where quotes from Generals of the past compliment current teachings in a beautiful way. Our hunger for more of God is satisfied by the depth and breadth of Dom's insight and the freshness and fearlessness of his political incorrectness – which is so needed.

Hugh and Ginny Cryer, Culture Changers

How hungry are you to experience more of God? Every time we have an encounter with our King, we are left with a deep longing for even more of Him! Because I know Dominic, I can assure you that these meditations were written from a life of deep intimacy with God. As you read each page, and read again, Dominic will take you deeper into discovering more of the presence, grace and love of God. And this discovery will transform you forever. Are you ready to boldly step out of religion and into a deeper love-relationship with the King? Then these devotions are just for you! Enjoy the journey.

Dr Francois Engelbrecht, Lead Pastor, Power House Ministries, Cape Town, South Africa

Dominic Muir doesn't just talk, he walks the walk of discipleship like few others. This book will be the greatest blessing to any who wish to live a life of active faith.

Duncan Barclay, Business Entrpreneur and CEO of Bizwinks

FOREWORD

A wonderful partnership of humility and hunger exists in the people who are authentically passionate about God. This hunger puts a profound demand on heaven itself. The results are astounding. Dominic's writing shines with the brilliance that comes from this partnership. He has a unique ability to make every word count. There is no fluff here – just one powerful sentence after another, filled with kingdom truth.

He has woven the Word of God, poignant quotes, and his personal discoveries, found in his quest for more of God, into a daily reminder of who God says we are.

I truly love and admire Dominic Muir. He is a contagious lover of Jesus – the kind of which I wish there were millions more. Perhaps with this book there will be. I encourage you to passionately read God Hunger and watch as God satisfies the cry of your heart.

Bill Johnson—Bethel Church, Redding, CA
Author of *When Heaven Invades Earth* and *God is Good*

"Pride must die in you, or nothing of heaven can live in you."
—Andrew Murray

DAY 1
INSIDE-OUT

—◦—

"Grace is but glory begun, and glory is but grace perfected ... As grace is first from God, so it is continually from him, as much as light is all day long from the sun, as well as at first dawn or at sun-rising."
—Jonathan Edwards

We live in a world dominated by an orphan spirit. It teaches people to be defensive, self-reliant, self-sufficient. It militates against the vulnerability and dependence called for by Father God as we take on His kingdom values.

We have been trained by an orphan world that says we must prove ourselves capable. This is a religious lie. We are not built for independence. In fact, the moment we decide to kill our independence, admit our own incapability, give up and look to the Father, is the moment of our greatest victory.

Resolutions and commitments to change our behaviour won't work. Allowing God to change our heart – and the subsequent outworking of that change affecting our behaviour – will transform us. Striving is the counterfeit of yielding. Religion attempts to transform us from the outside-in and does not work. The kingdom operates from the inside-out, and it does work, bringing about spiritual transformation.

In order to give up our self-reliance and yield to God's work in our life we need to learn humility. The orphan spirit is rooted in pride and control. It is offended by the prospect of making ourselves vulnerable. Yet, humble people cannot be humiliated or offended, because their self-focus has vanished, swallowed up by their love for God, themselves and others.

Perfectionism and control tend to produce only shame and fear. But when we are justified by Christ's perfection through faith in the finished work of the cross, He becomes our perfection. Suddenly, we are enough. We measure up. Slowly, our self-criticism and our judgement of others falls away, because we realise that everyone is significant. Let's get rid of our pride, because God resists the proud. Let's choose to go low and God will lift us up. Let's embrace the inside-out working of the Holy Spirit in our lives and look towards the glory that God desires to bring through His grace.

DAY 2
GRACE, UP CLOSE AND PERSONAL

———•———

"The sufficiency of my merit is to know that my merit is not sufficient."
—St Augustine

Did we get into God's kingdom by virtue of our own good works or merely through Jesus? The extent to which we understand our part in this process, I believe, determines the extent to which we will extend grace and mercy, both to ourselves and to those stuck in sin. The more we credit ourselves with inherent goodness, the less grace and mercy has a role to play!

But the degree to which we become uninhibited receptors of God's grace is the degree to which we can and will extend that grace to others.

Pope Francis said, "The proclamation of the saving love of God comes before moral and religious imperatives." In other words, when God looks at a person, He first sees someone whom He loves and wants unconditionally, before He is remotely concerned with their sin. Through the cross of Calvary God endorses, loves and invites every one of His children to heaven, before tripping over their sin, however vile it may be.

But even this does not adequately capture Francis' deeper insight – the priority of the person. This *personalism* with which God deals with us is one of the most radical aspects of the Christian faith. In every way that matters to God, human beings are completely equal and completely loved. They can't be reduced to ethical object lessons. Their dignity runs deeper than their failures. They matter more than any cause. They are the cause.

Put bluntly, to quote *The Prodigal*, "When you turn home, the Father kisses you through the pig crap before you shower!"

Grace is the empowering presence of God to do what only He can do. Grace doesn't excuse sin – it empowers righteousness. Grace is unmerited favour. Let's ask ourselves this question:

"How much unmerited favour can I afford to pay out today? How deep are my reserves?"

If we feel low on grace, we need only to return to the Source and ask to be refilled.

DAY 3
THE PRESSURE'S OFF

———•———

"Dear God, I am so afraid to open my clenched fists!
Who will I be when I have nothing left to hold on to?
Who will I be when I stand before you with empty hands?
Please help me to gradually open my hands and to discover
that I am not what I own, but what you want to give me."
—Henri Nouwen

The pressure to live well isn't on me or you. Jesus did it all and He lives in us. Grace works as we yield to Him, living in and through us.

Religion says, *Do ... achieve ... earn your validation ... justify your very existence ... the pressure is on you to perform...*

Jesus says, *Done ... accepted ... validated ... justified ... the pressure's off!*

The daily lot of those driven by religion is striving, anxiety and, ultimately, exhaustion and burn out. The inheritance of the child of God led by Christ's grace is freedom, joy and peace.

Those who fall back on self-reliance and their own resourcefulness to navigate life, who have taken on the principles of the world, unwittingly or otherwise, will know the daily pressure to perform and be dogged by a constant sense of failing to reach an acceptable standard. For those who are dead to self, humbled and dependent, the pressure is off. Yet we so easily succumb to the trap of trying to resume control of our lives. Author Larry Crabb expresses it well:

"We need to yield control over what happens in our lives and trust God to do whatever He thinks best ... until we develop a taste for God we prefer a better life of blessings from God over a better hope of intimacy with Him ... we prefer control over trust ... you were saved by grace and you'll grow by grace ... the law imposed the intolerable pressure to live perfectly in order to live well. You now stand in the Law of Liberty. Stand tall. Live as free men and women."

When praying and reflecting upon His ministry in John 17, Jesus said to His Father *"You have given me..."* twelve times. Jesus' humble dependence upon His Father is stunning and freeing at the same time. It reminds us that all we receive, we receive only by God's grace.

We live to play a role in God's story, not He in ours. He is God, we are not. He is central, we are peripheral. It's all about Him, not about us. There is freedom in this truth. The pressure is off!

DAY 4
HUMILITY VERSUS PRIDE

—•——

*"Don't push your way to the front; don't sweet-talk your way
to the top. Put yourself aside, and help others get ahead.
Don't be obsessed with getting your own advantage. Forget
yourselves long enough to lend a helping hand."*
(Philippians 2:3 MSG)

Pride blocks God out. Humility invites Him to come and help. Pride builds walls between people. Humility builds bridges.

Whenever we decide that someone has offended us, we are essentially deciding that we are superior to that person. Pride gets on its high horse. It erects a protective barrier with the thought that the culprit won't get inside our defences so easily next time. Pride turns its back and sulks away.

But humility steps forward, open handed, and moves towards the person, builds the bridge, seeks to understand and to offer grace.

One of the quickest routes into darkness is pride, offence and a sense of entitlement. The quickest route to receiving God's help is humility and surrender, which leads to His peace and joy.

One of the greatest weapons we have against pride is thankfulness. Thanksgiving to God in all circumstances is a good place to start. The Bible commands us to give thanks to God. Why? *Because if we are not thanking God, then we are not trusting Him.* We have become bogged down with self-entitlement.

Thanksgiving is the key which releases us from the claustrophobic confines of pride and offence into the spacious place of God's grace and freedom.

The truth is, we have no real rights. Every breath we breathe is a gift from God. Sometimes we become frustrated when things don't go our way, but the only way forward is to acknowledge, "You are God, I'm your child. You're the Potter, I'm the clay."

"When a man thinks he has got a good deal of strength, and is self-confident, you may look for his downfall. It may be years before it comes to light, but it is already commenced." (D.L. Moody)

Today God is calling you and I to relinquish our thirst for control and to choose to trust Him in the "midst of our mystery". We have to give up our right to be right if we want to experience the peace that surpasses all understanding.

DAY 5
ENTITLED?

———.———

"Rest and be thankful"
—William Wordsworth

In the beginning, in the Garden, we were not encumbered by the trap of comparison to others, or by feelings of insignificance, jealousy, envy, vanity or pride. Our focus and attention was fully upon God, our Father, and our glory covering was too thick for us to be aware of our nakedness. We were simply happy to be in a love relationship with our Father and one with another.

This freedom is our inheritance in Christ today. But the orphan spirit of Cain still strives to come to the fore, to bring an "offering" better than Abel's, and is consumed with the murderous thoughts of darkness. Orphans must succeed and prove themselves. Sons and daughters of God, however, stand approved by heaven, enjoying their relationship and working alongside their Father.

In Matthew 20:1-16 Jesus told a parable about the master of a house who hired a number of workers for his vineyard. Some laboured for several hours and others for a much shorter time, but they all got the same reward at the end. The workers who had toiled for longer immediately rose up with a sense of self-entitlement. "How come we didn't get paid more than those others?"

Jesus infers that it wasn't that the master didn't pay them a fair day's wage, rather they had fallen into the trap of comparing what they'd received with what the others had received. Jesus' simple, profound summary of this episode is,

"So the last will be first, and the first last" (Matthew 20:16)

The principle of the parable is that the Christian life is all grace from beginning to end. Jesus is the master in the parable, distributing grace generously to all. The workers who felt cheated received just as much grace as anyone else, but they measured it by worldly standards.

We live in an upside down kingdom that makes little sense to the worldly wise. The principles of God's kingdom have nothing to do with the principles of the world we've left behind. We must stop bringing all our "old ideas" to the table. There is nothing so wrong as the spirit which argues, "I have done this, therefore I expect something in return." God is not a celestial vending machine. We cannot manipulate Him. No matter what we do, we can never argue for our entitlement. Rather, in His presence we receive all the reward we could desire and more. His presence is full of joy, peace and satisfaction. Let's learn the art of thankfulness!

DAY 6
HUNGER FOR GOD

—·—

"If you don't feel strong desires for the manifestation of the glory of God, it is not because you have drunk deeply and are satisfied. It is because you have nibbled so long at the table of the world. Your soul is stuffed with small things, and there is no room for the great."
—John Piper

We all have a spiritual appetite as part of our makeup as human beings. In fact, this yearning for spiritual fulfilment is a constant in our daily life. The question is, where is our hunger being directed?

If we are not hungry for the presence and purposes of God, then you can be sure we are hungry for something else.

People chase after many things in response to this hunger: financial security, career success, the praise and affirmation of others, relationships, and more. But only Jesus can impart the abundance of life we crave. The more hungry for God we are, the more alive we are.

The revivalist John G. Lake said that the most powerful prayer any Christian can pray is, "God, make me hungry for you." We are all a product of our spiritual appetite and none of us is greater than our prayer life.

There is a healthy restlessness that each of us should embrace – the restlessness that longs for heaven, for a deeper knowledge of God's presence; the restlessness that marks us out as nothing more than pilgrims, passing through this temporary place and heading for our true destination.

Bill Johnson writes, "Never stop looking for His 'new thing'. The moment we think we have arrived, we will fall. The moment we lose that hunger to travel to find Him, the willingness to wait in line to hear Him, a humility to encounter Him in a package that offends us, we're in danger of missing His next move. Wise men still travel."

Stay hungry for God.

DAY 7
CONTROVERSY FOR THE SAKE OF TRUTH

————◆————

"Obviously I am not trying to win the approval of people,
but of God. If pleasing people were my goal, I would not be
Christ's servant."
(Galatians 1:10)

We live in a day when the righteous are continually being called upon to apologise – or worse still, are losing their jobs or being reprimanded by their employers simply for standing up for what they believe. Many cases have been reported in the press in recent times where Christians have come under fire for sticking to their beliefs.

Now more than ever, the people of God need to take a firm stand for the truth. Walter Martin said, "Controversy for the sake of truth is a divine command." The Gospel message is always offensive to those opposed to God's grace – that is what makes it controversial. But rather than siding with the politically correct who insist, "You can't say that..." – for the sake of the Gospel our posture should be, "We can't NOT say that!"

The fact that we deliver a message that, to some, is extremely uncomfortable, cannot dictate our degree of faithfulness. Our example is the Lord Jesus: forsaken, betrayed, ridiculed and in agony on the cross. His message was life and liberty to many, but to many it was also offensive in the extreme. He was hardly flavour of the month.

We too are commanded to speak the truth – for the sake of love, for the sake of Calvary. The muzzle must be removed from the crowd-pleasing Church. As the apostle Paul exhorts, *"If God is for us, who dare be against us."* Preach! Our obedience in proclaiming the undiluted Gospel – offensively good and offensively terrifying – both in the Church and in public, is honouring what Jesus endured for our sakes.

According to society it is both socially and politically unacceptable to say that Jesus is the only way to God – that we have found God for certain through Him alone, offering no concession to other "faiths". People will say we are being too narrow. But Jesus is very clear that "broad" spirituality *"leads to destruction"* and *"narrow is the way that leads to life."*

The truth is, we cannot have God and friendship with the world. Jesus made it clear that with the choice of His life would come hardship and persecution alongside joy and blessing. We are to rejoice in either scenario, because this is what produces spiritual fruit in our lives.

Let's stand for truth. Let's speak the truth in love. God is looking for people who won't sacrifice their anointing for mere respectability.

selah...

Relinquish – we block the work of God's grace in our lives until we come to the place of surrender. Once we relinquish control and admit our complete inability to live apart from the Holy Spirit's power, we begin flowing in the direction of God's river of grace.

Receive – the more we depend upon God, the more we will see His grace working in and through our lives. God doesn't pay His employees, He gives His children an inheritance they don't deserve.

Relish – there is nothing you or I can do to deserve God's blessing. Grace is not based on anything we do at all, but on what Christ has already done for us. We don't have to do anything to get blessed, we get abundance, for nothing (Romans 5:17)! The greatest blessing in life is becoming one who simply enjoys God. As the Westminster Shorter Catechism puts it: "Man's chief end is to glorify God, and to enjoy him forever."

Rest – religion thrives on earning the favour of God; grace tells us we already have it before we've done a single thing. Religion makes people feel proud when they succeed and guilty when they fail. Grace scandalously gives us what we don't deserve, yet our Father wants us to rest secure in this knowledge, living confidently out of our identity in Christ.

DAY 8
WHAT DO YOU SEE?

"Where there is no vision, the people perish."
(Proverbs 29:18)

God asks lots of questions in the Bible – not because He doesn't know the answers, but to ignite revelation in us. One question He regularly asks is, *"What do you see?"*

Ask yourself this question now. What is it that you see – for your life, your future, your ministry? If you don't see anything then ask God for His vision for your life. *"Ask, and it will be given to you"* (Matthew 7:7).

In the search for your unique calling and kingdom mandate, it might be helpful to consider the following:

1. What do you daydream about? God is a dreamer, a visionary, a creative being. When He created the earth I like to think that He began by dreaming and imagining what could be. What He saw in His heart He then birthed. Since we are made in God's image, we are wired the same way. What is it that you dream of doing with God's help?

2. What are you passionate about? Passion and excitement are indicators of God's purpose for your life. What is it that makes you really animated? Look to your passions for purpose.

3. What makes you angry? Righteous anger is also an indication of God's call. What inflames your emotions? Injustice, lack, poverty? Indeed, what do you hate? As Bill

Johnson writes, "What you hate tells me what you love." Has God called you to change something in society?

4. Pay attention to open doors and circumstantial evidence. Often God will make His will clear by opening or closing doors. "A man's heart plans his way, But the Lord directs his steps" (Proverbs 16:9).

5. Listen to wise counsel. Henri Nouwen said that, "Deep friendship is a calling forth of each other's chosen-ness." If we are wise, we will be alert to hearing God's voice, not just on our own, but through His saints. It keeps us humble and nurtures the interdependency of the body of Christ.

6. Keep moving forward. If, for now, you are not sure what it is that God has called you to do, just keep walking forward and He will direct you.

7. Once you have "seen", focus on God's power, not yours. It has been said that any vision that seems achievable is likely not from God. Once you see it, depend entirely on the power of our mighty God to see it accomplished.

DAY 9
TRUE HUMILITY

———·———

"Pride must die in you, or nothing of heaven can live in you."
—Andrew Murray

We must have a big God and a big destiny or else have false humility. False humility is a form of pride because it is utterly self-conscious.

By contrast, true humility is God-conscious. It is focused on the greatness and magnificence of the Lord and therefore puts our own abilities and achievements into their true perspective.

True humility is having an absolute, helpless, childlike dependence on Him to make us into everything He has ordained.

False humility limits God to man's vision. Worse still, it leads us to hide in the shadows and shirk our God-ordained responsibility and calling. When God calls us, to respond by saying, "I can't do that" means that our focus is in the wrong place. It's on us rather than Him!

True humility is knowing that through our flesh we can achieve nothing of eternal consequence, but with God's power He will do, "exceedingly abundantly above all that we ask or think, according to the power that works in us" (Ephesians 3:20).

As Jesus said, "I am the vine, you are the branches. He who abides in Me, and I in him, bears much fruit; for without Me you can do nothing" (John 15:5).

Like Paul, we too can say, "I can do all things through Christ who strengthens me" (Philippians 4:13).

DAY 10
GODLY VERSUS SELFISH AMBITION

"For where envy and self-seeking exist, confusion and every evil thing are there."
(James 3:16)

"Almost every sinful action ever committed can be traced back to a selfish motive. It is a trait we hate in other people but justify in ourselves."
—Stephen Kendrick, *The Love Dare*

There is a need for us to discern between godly and selfish ambition. We must hunger and thirst for the name of Jesus to be glorified; to build His kingdom and not our own. In this respect we must always be ready to lay down and give away anything that God has not asked us to build.

Graham Cooke says, "God doesn't measure our success by what we achieve – by results and statistics. God measures our success by the faithfulness we display."

Dr Martin Luther King Jr. wrote, "If a man is called to be a street sweeper, he should sweep even as Michelangelo painted or Beethoven composed music or Shakespeare wrote poetry. He should sweep streets so well that all the host of heaven and earth will pause to say, here lived a great street sweeper who did his job well."

In heaven there is no sacred/secular divide; all is worship. What will be significant in eternity is not what we did, but the degree to which we were obedient to the Lord and were motivated by love.

Bill Johnson writes, "We are never significant because we want to be, we are significant because we do what He says.

Pure simple obedience. No one on earth may even know your name but heaven records your victories ... Heaven has a different way of looking at stuff."

Stop grading what you do for God and just do.

"Spontaneously and without effort we have fulfilled the law ... by loving our neighbour as ourselves. It is an image, a foretaste, of what we must become to all if Love Himself rules in us without a rival." (C.S. Lewis, *The Four Loves*)

DAY 11
CALLED TO PURPOSE

——•——

"If our value before God is defined by what we do ... then
we land in a very deep pitfall ... we need to realise that our
value comes from deciding to embrace the cross and its
manifestation in our lives. Nothing else."
—Shawn Bolz

God has called each of us with a specific purpose and given
us the grace necessary to fulfil it. Some people speak about
the subject of "calling" as though it is very mysterious and
difficult to discover. Not so, because the Bible is very clear
about our fundamental purpose on earth.

Thomas Merton wrote, "Before the Lord wills me to do
anything, He first of all wills me to 'be.' What I do must depend
on what I am." First and foremost God has predestined us to
conform to the image and likeness of His Son, Jesus (Romans
8:29). "Success isn't a place to reach, but a state of being,"
writes Steve Backlund. Alongside this, God has set in a
place a "prosperous" plan for our lives (Jeremiah 29:11) and
preordained our days (Psalm 139:16).

A recent piece of research from medical practitioners
indicated that the majority of their patients suffered from a
profound lack of purpose in their lives. In other words, apart
from continuing to do the expected things – family, work,
social life – their lives had no overarching goal; their goals
were pretty meaningless. This in turn had an effect on their
health and wellbeing. We realise from the Bible, however,
that God has given each of us the opportunity to walk in His
perfect plan for our life, bringing heaven to earth and living
purposefully.

"For you did not receive the spirit of bondage again to fear, but you received the Spirit of adoption by whom we cry out, 'Abba, Father.' The Spirit Himself bears witness with our spirit that we are children of God." (Romans 8:15-16)

"We love Him because He first loved us." (1 John 4:19)

This means that our primary calling is rooted in our identity – to become a beloved child of God. Rooted in that place of love and acceptance, we are given the "greatest commandment" (Matthew 22:38) to worship and love God with every breath we breathe. Only then can we begin to fulfil the second great command to love our neighbour as ourselves.

If you are searching for your "calling", focus on the high calling of loving God and enjoying Him forever.

DAY 12
HOW WILL THEY HEAR?

——•——

*"What marvel the devil does not love field preaching!
Neither do I; I love a commodious room, a soft cushion, a
handsome pulpit. But where is my zeal, if I do not trample all
these underfoot in order to save one more soul?"*
—John Wesley

Jesus said, *"Whatever I tell you in the dark, speak in the light;
and what you hear in the ear, preach on the housetops"*
(Matthew 10:27-28). Paul reminds us in Romans 10:14, *"How
then shall they call on Him in whom they have not believed?
And how shall they believe in Him of whom they have not
heard? And how shall they hear without a preacher?"*

When we realise the depth of the love God that has poured
out upon us, we are compelled by love to reach out to others
– the broken, hurting, lonely or simply lost.

Fewer and fewer people in the western world are part of
a church. As uncomfortable as this may sound, this should
translate into the fact that more and more millions of
people are destined to populate hell. Multitudes of today's
generation have no interest in church, nor see its relevance to
their lives. The TV and print media don't preach the Gospel.
So how will people hear about Jesus and be drawn to Him?

It's not popular to talk like this, but the fact is, Jesus'
commission to the Church is radically different from what
most of us see and experience in church culture today. Yet,
we have a duty to obey the word of God and we will be
accountable to Him in due course.

It is our calling to take the good news about Christ into
our workplaces, marketplaces, and the homes of our

communities, compelled by love. To that end we must return to a bold proclamation of the truth. Jesus paints a vivid picture of seeking out the lost in the places they have wandered off into:

"What man of you, having a hundred sheep, if he loses one of them, does not leave the ninety-nine in the wilderness, and go after the one which is lost until he finds it? ... There will be more joy in heaven over one sinner who repents than over ninety-nine just persons who need no repentance." (Luke 15:4,7)

We need to seek out those who are lost. Share the love and peace of Christ with them. Speak out our faith. Preach the gospel. Offer prayer. Always be ready!

DAY 13
THE TRUTH ABOUT GOD THE FATHER

"The right way to approach God is to stretch out our hands and ask of One who we know has the heart of a Father."
— Dietrich Bonhoeffer, *The Cost of Discipleship*

While I appreciate that each person reading this will each have a different experience and understanding of what "father" means to them, in God we have a perfect Father (Matthew 5:48). Where earthly fathers are imperfect, our Heavenly Father loves us perfectly and completely. The great revivalist Jonathan Edwards wrote, "Of all the knowledge that we can ever obtain, the knowledge of God, and the knowledge of ourselves, are the most important." Indeed, the knowledge of ourselves springs from our right understanding of our heavenly Father. Think about the following truths and confess them over yourself – because they are true!

My Father loves me unconditionally. He loved me first – I am His beloved and cherished child.

My Father is pleased with me. In Christ I'm perfect and priceless, irrespective of my behavior or performance!

My Father is my provider, my healer, my protector and my deliverer.

My Father is my encourager and comforter.

My Father is the Almighty God and is for me, in me, with me, behind me, working through me and cheering me on! If God is for me, who cares who's against me?

My Father is full of mercy and grace and has both for me in abundance every day.

My Father is good all the time and His thoughts towards me are always good, full of hope and for a good future.

My Father is faithful and trustworthy – the most trustworthy individual in the universe.

My Father is true – it is impossible for Him to lie; He is kind; He is patient, slow to anger, rich in love and full of compassion (Exodus 34:6).

My Father is sovereign. He's not surprised by me or anything that has happened in my life.

My Father created me, chose me and ordained me. I didn't create myself, think me up, or choose Him. He knew what He was getting into! My Father is all-knowing, ever-present. It is impossible for Him to abandon me.

My Father is my good shepherd leading me in His wise plan for my life. His purpose will not take me where His grace cannot sustain me.

DAY 14
GOD IS GOOD, ALL THE TIME

—·—

"The root of all sin is the suspicion that God is not good"
—Oswald Chambers

The author Brennan Manning wrote that if we, "took the love of all the best mothers and fathers who ever lived – all the goodness, kindness, patience, fidelity, wisdom, tenderness, strength and love – and united all those virtues in one person, that person would only be a faint shadow of the love and mercy in the heart of God for you and me."

When something bad happens in our lives, it is very tempting for us to question, "God, are you *really* good? Can I truly trust and rest in you?" If we doubt God's goodness and move out of that place of rest, however, we will quickly move into self-effort. In other words, we will begin to try to persuade God by our actions to be good to us in the way that we want. And then we have missed the whole point!

The truth is, no matter what happens to us in this fallen world, we have a God who is sovereign and knows exactly what He's doing. When things don't go according to plan we must continue to trust. We can't take matters into our own hands and attempt to manipulate God into blessing us.

It is so tempting to want to take control. But when we are in control the pressure is on *us*. When we relinquish control to Jesus, the yoke, the pressure, is on Him. He is responsible for our lives, since we are entirely dependent upon Him. We simply have the privilege and joy of co-labouring with Him!

Although such radical trust can seem counterintuitive (and is certainly counter-cultural), it is the path towards real peace and fulfilment.

"Trust in the Lord with all your heart, and lean not on your own understanding." (Proverbs 3:5)

If you doubt at all that God is maybe too busy or too distracted with bigger issues to be concerned with the things that are important to you, soak in this beautiful, scriptural extrapolation from J.I. Packer:

"I am graven on the palms of His hands. I am never out of His mind. All my knowledge of Him depends on His sustained initiative in knowing me. I know Him, because He first knew me, and continues to know me. He knows me as a friend, One who loves me; and there is no moment when His eye is off me, or His attention distracted from me, and no moment, therefore, when His care falters."

selah...

"Great thoughts of your sin alone
will drive you to despair; but great
thoughts of Christ will pilot you into
the haven of peace."
—Charles Spurgeon

"I'd like to propose to you that revelation is not the product of laborious study, but it is the fruit of friendship with God."
—Kris Vallotton

DAY 15
THROUGH THE DESERT

——·——

"We must through many tribulations
enter the kingdom of God."
(Acts 14:22)

Every person used greatly of/by God in the Bible went through a personal wilderness – one that shaped their character and enabled them to fulfil their destiny. Abraham, Jacob, Joseph, Moses, David, Paul – they were each tested in the desert (some literally, others figuratively) and sanctified by God.

The desert experience wasn't an attack of the enemy, it was God's doing. He led them through it, not in spite of but because of His goodness, mercy and love. God's commitment to our receiving His abundant life means that we might need our character refined as we hide in a cave or languish in a prison. Paul speaks of his trials thus:

"Now I want you to know, brothers and sisters, that what has happened to me has actually served to advance the gospel. As a result, it has become clear throughout the whole palace guard and to everyone else that I am in chains for Christ. And because of my chains, most of the brothers and sisters have become confident in the Lord and dare all the more to proclaim the gospel without fear." (Philippians 1:12-14)

If we try to avoid the desert, then we sacrifice character, courage and spiritual power. There is a dangerous form of teaching in the body of Christ that would suggest that because Jesus went to the cross, we don't have to pick up ours. In other words, if as a Christian I am suffering, something is wrong.

But Paul clearly states that if we are children of God, then we are heirs: *"heirs of God and joint heirs with Christ, if indeed we suffer with Him…"* (Romans 8:17) Even Jesus *"though He was a Son, yet He learned obedience by the things which He suffered"* (Hebrews 5:8). Adversity introduces a man to himself. So don't waste your trials!

There is an equally dangerous teaching that defames God of His innate and miraculous goodness and promotes Him as the author of sickness as a means of disciplining us. Sickness is not the desert that God ordains. Bill Johnson writes, "It is inconsistent to have Jesus pay a price for healing and for us to believe it is not God's intention to heal." As Jesus clarified, *"If a house is divided against itself, that house cannot stand."* (Mark 3:25)

"You don't really know Jesus is all you need until Jesus is all you have," writes Tim Keller. "…Suffering is actually at the heart of the Christian story" (*Walking with God Through Pain and Suffering*). The truth is, the cross of Christ gives us salvation, healing and deliverance, by grace and through faith alone. But our personal "cross" gets us our destiny; it forms Christ in us.

Take some time to meditate on this beautiful metaphor from Watchman Nee: "The breaking of the alabaster box and the anointing of the Lord filled the house with the odour, with the sweetest odour. Everyone could smell it. Whenever you meet someone who has really suffered; been limited, gone through things for the Lord, been willing to be imprisoned by the Lord, just being satisfied with Him and nothing else, immediately you sense the fragrance. There is a savour of the Lord. Something has been crushed, something has been broken, and there is a resulting odour of sweetness."

On the other side of the wilderness lies the promised land. We must embrace the cross of Christ but also take up our cross daily, dying to self and eschewing the comfort of complacency. A Church without true discipleship is emasculated, robbed of its authority.

It's time to embrace the challenge. Do we want to be entertained and follow a Christian faith that makes us happy alone? Or do we want to follow the way of the cross that ultimately leads to unsearchable glory and unfathomable joy – even though at times the road may be a hard one?

"More than that, we rejoice in our sufferings, knowing that suffering produces endurance, and endurance produces character, and character produces hope..." (Romans 5:3-4)

DAY 16
THE LAW OF LONGEVITY

"An inheritance gained hastily at the beginning will not be blessed at the end."
(Proverbs 20:21)

The apostle Paul wrote much about perseverance and endurance and how they both work to produce character and how character leads to hope (Romans 5:3-4). Through Jesus we are saved, by faith, and He has won for us a glorious eternal inheritance.

But until the day that inheritance is fully ours, we are on a journey – and that journey has its challenges. There is much joy, but there is also some difficulty and pain. What keeps us going, despite life's ups and downs?

Hope.

With hope we persevere; and perseverance produces more hope. That's why James also encourages us to embrace, even celebrate, our adverse experiences.

"Count it all joy when you fall into various trials, knowing that the testing of your faith produces patience. But let patience have its perfect work, that you may be perfect and complete, lacking nothing." (James 1:2-4)

The point of Paul and James' teaching is this: anything that comes cheaply will not last. If we embrace His process in us we are made ready to handle His promise for us. Patience, formed through trial is needed for us to take hold of our destiny. *"By faith and patience we inherit the promises"* (Hebrews 6:12).

Character, which comes through perseverance, is needed to sustain the promise when it comes. There is no cheap solution; no six steps to success. Look at the example of Jesus:

"Though He was a Son, yet He learned obedience by the things which He suffered." (Hebrews 5:8)

If even Jesus suffered in order to learn obedience to His heavenly Father, then so must we. This is not a popular message in today's consumerist, have-it-all culture. And yet, it is the path to true joy, true fulfilment, true peace. Through patient endurance Father God is forming Christ in you and me. And as the writer of Ecclesiastes put it,

"He has made everything beautiful in its time." (Ecclesiastes 3:11)

God is busy shaping us for eternity. He alone is wise. He knows what He's doing.

DAY 17
SWORD PRACTICE

—·—

"Be diligent to present yourself approved to God, a worker
who does not need to be ashamed, rightly dividing the word
of truth."
(2 Timothy 2:15)

With so much technology available at our fingertips, we have
never had so many ways in which we can read the Bible –
nor so many distractions that would pull us away from it.
Smartphones and tablets all have free Bible apps and there is
a plethora of Bible versions and study resources on the web.
But our fast-flowing sound-bite information age means that
we need to apply serious focus in order to spend time with
God in His word, absorbing His truth, becoming His truth, so
that our lives are transformed.

I can scarcely emphasise enough the importance of
knowing the Bible thoroughly, but we must also learn to
wield it correctly as the Sword of the Spirit (Ephesians 6:17).
It is our best defence against all the schemes of the enemy.

Charles Spurgeon, commenting on Ephesians six writes,
"To be a Christian is to be a warrior. The good soldier of
Jesus Christ must not expect to find ease in this world: it is a
battlefield. Neither must he reckon upon the friendship of the
world; for that would be enmity against God. His occupation
is war ... You are to grasp your weapon and go forth to fight
... The one note that rings out from the text is this: take the
sword of the spirit! Take the word of God! No longer is it talk
and debate! No longer is it parley and compromise! The word
of thunder is – 'Take the sword.' The Captain's voice is clear as
a trumpet."

Without the continued presence of God's truth in our lives, subtle deceptions can begin to creep in. The truth is, without the stabilising influence of the word we soon tend towards worldly, liberal minded thinking – like a ship without a rudder. Vague theology paves the way for absolute truths to be sacrificed on the altar of human reasoning and human pleasing.

Every believer needs to be a lover of God's Word, a lover of the truth. But remember: the Word of God is a person, Jesus. We must know Him, love Him, sleep with Him, and devour His Scripture in the presence of His Holy Spirit. We must call regularly on the Spirit of wisdom and revelation, counsel and knowledge. For the Word is the gateway to our freedom (John 8:31), faith (Romans 10:17), truth and sanctification (John 17:17) and is useful for correction and training in righteousness (2 Timothy 3:16).

Absolute truth is unpopular in today's world which so cherishes political correctness and relativism, yet we must uphold the truth. Otherwise we will fall into a man-fearing, diluted, comfort-zone type of Christianity that has the appearance of godliness without its power (2 Timothy 3:5).

Hebrews 4:12 says,

"For the word of God is living and powerful, and sharper than any two-edged sword, piercing even to the division of soul and spirit, and of joints and marrow, and is a discerner of the thoughts and intents of the heart."

We, the Church, need to be armed with the Sword. Like a good soldier, make sure that you make time each day to put in some Sword practice.

DAY 18
SHIFTING OUR FOCUS

———•———

"We do this by keeping our eyes on Jesus, the champion who initiates and perfects our faith."
(Hebrews 12:2 NLT)

Smartphone, iPad, laptop, desktop, TV – there's a size for every occasion. Screen time is a big deal. There are so many options for staying "connected" that people are hardly away from their screens unless they are asleep. But while social media platforms such as Facebook have allowed us to be in contact with friends and family all over the world, many people lead lives of "quiet desperation" whilst portraying to the world a totally false view of their life.

For many, the screen is a way of suspending reality, escaping our pain, taking back control and presenting the life we wished we were living – airbrushing out the wrinkles and scars in the process. Don't get me wrong, I have a Facebook profile. I enjoy staying in the loop with friends, celebrating life and I love to use it to preach the gospel! I'm not advocating a mass exodus from social media. But, used in the wrong way, there are some negative effects of social media that we should all be concerned about.

1. Identity crisis. Jesus said, "Where your treasure is, there your heart will follow." The more we invest in social media, the more we will submit to its values and appetite. You only have to look at the endless stream of "selfies" filling your news feed – as though an event never actually happened unless we snapped a picture of ourselves at the scene. We will also suffer from submitting to the way social media defines identity. The temptation to present a perfectly manicured self-image and a life full of excitement and high points is unsustainable. The drive to rack up "likes" is empty and will never satisfy. There is only one place of sure approval, justification and love – the Father's embrace. The current obsession with self flies in the face of our identity and freedom in Christ alone.

2. *Relational erosion.* We were created for intimacy. For all that social media has achieved in connecting people all over the world, it seems to be undermining relationships as a result. Never have we been so connected, yet so alone. People are being pulled away from building real, empathic and intimate relationships. A great many of our connections with people online are highly tenuous. How much time do we spend investing into authentic, face-to-face, real-time relationships? We need to let go of our need for "virtual" control and learn to be fully present with and fully seen by each other again. Emanuel, another name for Jesus, means God with us.

3. *Always on.* Paul Tillich writes, "Loneliness expresses the pain of being alone and solitude expresses the glory of being alone." Blaise Pascal went so far as to say that all the evils in the world arise from man not being able to sit in a room alone. I have spoken already about the plethora of options for "staying connected". The truth is, the Internet has our attention for a great deal of our time. But as a result of this pervasive cultural current of distraction (and often counterfeit worship) we have become a restless, joyless and a lonely people. How does the time we spend online affect our

relationship with God? Our 24-7, always available, connected world means that the foremost connection we need – with our heavenly Father – is hard to come by. It can be squeezed out of our life completely unless we are intentional about finding a place of solitude and stillness where we can rest in God's presence, hear Him speak and get our joy back (Psalm 16:11).

This generation more than any other needs to be aggressively purposeful about pursuing the presence of God, managing their online life so that it does not manage them. Set boundaries. Let your life reflect Christ. Be authentic. "Own" the platforms you use – let them add nothing to your identity.

DAY 19
STRANGERS

"These men of faith ... saw it all awaiting them on ahead and were glad, for they agreed that this earth was not their real home but that they were just strangers visiting down here."
(Hebrews 11:13 TLB)

John Wesley said, "We ought to live every day as though we've come out of another world into this world — but with the power of that world still upon us. We should live and speak and move in that power, and have our whole being in Jesus Christ!"

When we are in Christ, we are called to live like strangers in this world. We are present in it, yet we are like foreign diplomats who belong to an entirely different kingdom, who have been dispatched here to perform a specific mission. We may have to live within the framework of this land, but ultimately we are subject to a higher authority.

Many people live lives that are governed by their environment and the circumstances in which they find themselves. Our English word "circumstance" finds its origin in Latin and literally means "that which surrounds us". As believers who are learning each day to walk in the Spirit, we find that we can live life two ways:

1. We can live in reaction to the things that surround us – our culture, our circumstances, the example of the lives of others – and be defined by those things.

Or,

2. We can live from an inner source of faith, hope and love and allow those fruits of the Spirit to shape and define us.

When we live from the inside out, as carriers of the presence of God, we find that our reaction to our "surroundings" in life is entirely different. We are no longer blown about by our circumstances, but rather led by the gentle wind of the Spirit. Circumstances submit to Christ in us. No longer are our lives like thermometers; we become thermostats – atmospheres change around us.

Born again Christians are a new race of people, seated in a new realm (1 Peter 2:9, Ephesians 2:6). We are beyond human (1 Corinthians 3:3). We are to live differently to those around us. Most people cling onto the fabric of their lives – people, possessions, self-worth, self-image – because they have nothing else apart from the here-and-now. Instead, we are to live as pilgrims. The material aspect of our world need have no grip on us, because we are on a journey to a better place. We have our eyes fixed on our eternal destination. Here are four indications that your Christian pilgrimage is maturing:

- You carry increasing joy outside of circumstantial blessing
- You walk in deepening trust outside of circumstantial control
- Your desire to see people saved far outweighs your desire to stay safe
- You are less concerned about "me" and more concerned about serving God and others

Remember today that the "here and now" is not your final destination. You are here, but actually you don't belong, because you are a citizen of another kingdom – the kingdom of God.

DAY 20
LOOKING IN THE RIGHT DIRECTION

———.———

"So then, let us rid ourselves of everything that gets in the way, and of the sin which holds on to us so tightly, and let us run with determination the race that lies before us. 2 Let us keep our eyes fixed on Jesus, on whom our faith depends from beginning to end."
(Hebrews 12:2 GNT)

I have heard it said that Formula 1 drivers are trained to focus only on where they want to go. They travel so fast in their high performance cars that if they look at something for more than a split second they will veer towards it. As one instructor put it, "Don't look at anything you don't want to hit!"

In our spiritual lives it's important to keep our eyes looking in the right direction. What we focus on, the thing or things that are always getting our attention – that is effectively what we will worship. It seems that we humans can't simply turn off our worship – we are always worshipping someone or something. So we need to make sure that we are pointing in the right direction. We need to make sure that Jesus is the focus of our attention and Father God the object of our worship.

T.L. Osborn said, "The vision you hold is the promise of what will unfold in your life."

In simple terms, you'll only ever be as big as your vision of God.

Henry David Thoreau put a slightly different spin on this saying, "It's not what you look at that matters, it's what you see."

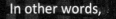

In other words,

What fills our vision? Where is our attention focused? What keeps on catching our eye distracting us?

Distraction is a key weapon of our enemy. The temptation to sin outright can be clumsy and obvious, so often he settles for keeping us occupied with trivia, distracted from our mission – but therefore just as ineffective.

With our eyes fixed on Jesus we will not be distracted. We will not go crashing into those things in life that have the potential to either derail or destroy us. As Rick Warren writes concerning life's "race": "I want you to make it to the finish line ... to endure the unendurable you must see the invisible – Jesus."

DAY 21
LIVING FROM KINGDOM VALUES

———·———

"True godliness does not turn men out of the world, but
enables them to live better in it and excites their endeavours
to mend it."
—William Penn

Over the next few days I want us to reflect on how we choose
to live in light of this great salvation. Living from kingdom of
God values will form the bedrock of a Christ-centred life.

First, some context: the western world is primarily task-
oriented, driven by results. The means are easily justified
by the end. This driven-ness is often at the expense of our
integrity, healthy family life, authentic relationships and a
selfless, agenda-less love for God. At the root of this malaise
is the orphan-hearted need to be justified before God and
man by works. If we are not careful, we can allow this restless
driven-ness to get things done – the idolatry of doing and
achieving, even when it's for a kingdom vision – to taint our
motives and supersede the importance of simply living in
God's presence.

The world and religion look at the outside of the cup. Both
are obsessed with superficial appearance and activity. But
God looks at the heart, the motives, the "how" and "why" of
our life choices.

This is where our values come in. Values underpin the
"how" of life. They are the culture within which destiny is
formed, grown and lived out. Proverbs 23:7 says, *"As a man
thinks in his heart so is he."* Values are held in our hearts. They
are not a set of dry regulations, or dead rituals copied from

a dusty book, but are formed in relationship with God as we follow Jesus and allow Him to change our hearts. Kingdom values help us to live intentionally and powerfully from God's heart, instead of passively, as victims to the patterns and demands of the world around us (Romans 12:2).

Living from kingdom values establishes integrity, builds character and cultivates a healthy consistency in all areas of life. It makes us the same person on the inside as the outside; the same person in the office, the supermarket, when no one's looking, as we are in church. The sacred/secular divide is gone. Powerful and self-controlled people cultivate healthy boundaries to protect the values from which they live. When we say "yes" to some things, we inevitably say "no" to others. Seth Dahl puts it like this: "It's not hard to make decisions once you know what your values are."

The simple values in the chapters following, such as intimacy with God, trust and rest, and more, are like lights that will illuminate our way and provide a firm foundation, as we seek to walk with Christ.

Take a moment to write down the values you grew up with, the culture and priorities that were passed down to you, consciously or subconsciously, by your family, education and friends. Do these line up with the word of God? Ask the Lord to show you any ungodly values in your life. Now write down some values on which you want to base the rest of your life. You may find a marked difference!

DAY 22
KINGDOM VALUES 1

1. Intimacy with God. Before I have any other communication with anyone, my day starts with the Lord. There is a reason why the first commandment – which Jesus singled out as being of prime importance – gets us to focus completely on Father God and worship Him alone. This way we are able to relate to others from a safe and solid foundation, from a place of unconditional love, grace and wisdom.

Our lives are, first and foremost, lived for Him. Our main task in life is simply to get to know Him more. As we put Him first, He delights in pouring out His love and power through us, so that it touches the lives of others. Jesus spoke about our essential need for connection with Him – like the branches of a vine, drawing life from their source. From this place of connection, of abiding in Him, we yield rest, peace, intimacy and lasting fruit.

2. Trust and Rest. Trust is a daily posture that believes that God will father us, love us and guide us better than we can do those things ourselves – because no one knows us like Him and no one loves us more than Him. Why should we trust God? Because He is the author of goodness (Matthew 19:17; James 1:17), the epicentre of knowledge, wisdom and power (Romans 16:27, Matthew 19:26), and the incarnation of love itself (1 John 4:16).

When we trust in God we rest from strife and anxiety. Anxiety is, really, the fight to stay in control. Trust lets go of control and yields peaceful rest. We rest in the certainty that God is a good and perfect Father (Matthew 5:48) whose happy responsibility it is to lead us in His plan of righteousness (Psalm 23, John 10); who is always looking forward to spending time with us (Mark 3:14, John 17:21); who is always for us (Romans 8:31) and is always in a good mood, irrespective of how we are. He can fix anything anytime and works everything out for our good (Romans 8:28).

We can choose to trust God at all times (Psalm 62:8), even if we are not sure exactly what is going on (Proverbs 3:5). Indeed, authentic trust must regularly embrace mystery. The bottom line is: God is looking for hearts that are fully His, so He can show Himself strong on their behalf! (2 Chronicles 16:9)

KINGDOM VALUES 2

——·——

"The time you spend alone with God will transform your character and increase your devotion. Then your integrity and godly behaviour in an unbelieving world will make others long to know the Lord."
—Charles Stanley

3. Identity. Many people fight a lifelong battle to find and hold onto their self-worth. In Christ, that fruitless search is completely diffused, because our value and significance is not determined by our self-effort, nor by the opinions of others, but by what God says about us and what He did for us. Value is ultimately determined by what someone is willing to pay. We are simply loved and accepted by God through our Lord Jesus because He gave His life for us at Calvary (Romans 8:32). The fact that we are fully known and fully loved by God makes us significant. Our value is intrinsic, not earned.

We cannot afford to entertain thoughts or opinions about our identity that are not in the heart of God. Paul wrote, "the carnal mind is enmity against God" (Romans 8:7). Bill Johnson puts it like this: "The mind is either at war with God or it is being renewed. There is no middle ground." Gideon's mind was the biggest block to his nation-delivering mantel; not his enemies, but the way Gideon saw himself. Be very careful that your thoughts line up with what God is saying O mighty person of valour!

The truth is, God is patient and kind towards us (Galatians 5:22; 1 Corinthians 13:4), so we should be patient and kind to ourselves. God loves us unconditionally, so we should love and accept ourselves. God doesn't condemn us (Romans 8:1), so we should not condemn ourselves – either by our attitudes or by speaking harsh words about ourselves. If we do, we are contradicting the Lord!

God wants each of us to live free from expectation, control and performance, and instead embrace His freedom (John 8:32). We are free from the law of sin and death! (Romans 8:2) This way of living releases us from captivity and into our destiny. It is only when we cease from our restless doing that we discover what is to be done. As John Piper says, "God is most glorified in us when we are most satisfied in Him."

As a pilgrim, I am learning to think the way God thinks and talk the way God talks. The Bible says that the more I agree with God and allow His truth to permeate my thinking (the essence of repentance) and to destroy demonic strongholds and arguments (2 Corinthians 10:3-5), the more I will be "transformed" (Romans 12:2) to walk in joy, peace, hope, freedom – God's perfect will for my life (John 8:30-32, Romans 15:13). That's a heady inheritance! Meditate on these truths about your identity in Christ as you go about your day:

- You are fearfully and wonderfully made for a specific purpose (Psalm 139:14-16, 2 Timothy 1:9), so embrace the uniqueness of who God made you to be

- God has declared you worthy to receive all of His blessings in Christ (Ephesians 1:3)

- God enjoys and delights in you (Zephaniah 3:17; Psalm 147:11; Psalm 18:19)

KINGDOM VALUES 3

"Jesus calls us to his rest, and meekness is His method. The meek man cares not at all who is greater than he, for he has long ago decided that the esteem of the world is not worth the effort."
—A.W. Tozer, Pursuit of God

4. Love and Service. The Christ-follower is not egocentric or inward looking, but Christ-focused and other-centric. Fashioned by the One who is the embodiment of love, we are made to love Him and others; to live to serve. We are not meant to be isolated beings – God created us for intimacy with Him and interdependence with others. We must seek to live with authenticity, transparency and vulnerability. In short, our goal in life should be to love the One, and to love the one in front of us. We are truly free when we live to serve, give honour, and prefer others above ourselves.

Rooted in the security of Jesus' love, our life is not about what we do, but who we are. There is such security in knowing that we have nothing to prove – we are accepted by our Father, completely and wholly. In the same way that Jesus rebuked the Pharisees' "whitewashed" lifestyles and rituals, God is more interested in our heart than our deeds. We work from a place of relational communion with our God, not task-driven achievement. Is love for God and others the driving force of my life?

5. Word-centred. Our lives must be built on the word of God. The more we absorb the word, the clearer we will hear God's voice and the more we will be changed by its transforming truth. The word of God has to be the foundation of our lives, otherwise we are building on sinking sand (Matthew 7:24-27). The truth of God's word, and His promises spoken over us, provide heaven's blueprint for kingdom living.

6. Embracing the journey. Our lives are not about who we were in our past, or even who we are today, as much as who we are choosing to become. We are in process; we're on a journey to become increasingly more like Jesus. There is no limit to the transformation available in our lives, because there is no limit to how much our minds can be renewed (Romans 12:2) or how much of the Lord we can discover:

"And we all, who with unveiled faces contemplate the Lord's glory, are being transformed into his image with ever-increasing glory, which comes from the Lord, who is the Spirit." (2 Corinthians 3:18)

The various seasons and trials of life help to shape our character and to "form Christ in us" (Galatians 4:19). God's power is made perfect in our weakness. There is purpose in the tests we face because they build perseverance, which the Bible says leads to character and ultimately hope. Every test, inconvenience and place of humbling is an opportunity to decide who we are going to become. God, the potter, knows exactly what He is doing with this clay. Our responsibility is to remain soft in His masterful hands.

DAY 25
KINGDOM VALUES 4

———•———

7. Humility. Humility is not thinking of ourselves as any better or any worse than others, but thinking of ourselves less. Humble people are those with a realistic self-view. To be humble is to acknowledge that without Jesus we can do nothing. Humility means that we open ourselves to the feedback and loving correction of other believers. Humility means that we treat every person we come across with the same excellence and honour. Humility means that we look for the "gold" in others, and celebrate their victories. We refuse to speak negatively of others or judge their lives. Truly humble people can't be humiliated because their pride can no longer be offended.

8. Thankfulness. Michael Ramsden said, "We are not made happy in life by what we acquire but by what we appreciate." The secret of being thankful is learning to see everything from the Father's perspective. Knowing that our Father is committed to providing for all of our needs, we can rejoice always and live in thankfulness. We are called to lives of gratitude and royal generosity. Sin is essentially a failure of gratitude. We sin because we do not fully grasp who God is and what He has done for us.

When we understand just how committed God is to caring for His children, we can dispel the poverty mentality that besets so many, keeping them prisoners to fear. We should have no fear of lack, for we "shall not want" (Psalm 23). Our Father has unlimited resources at His disposal and has made it clear that everything that is His is ours (Luke 15:31).

With a renewed mind, thankfulness comes very easily!

9. Self-control. Self-control is perhaps the least spoken about fruit of the Spirit, and yet it is so crucial for living a godly, peace-filled life. Self-controlled people are powerful people because they know how to say "yes" or "no" in order to protect their God-given mandate. Yielding to the Holy Spirit allows us to dismiss false comforts, to observe healthy boundaries and to learn to live from divinely inspired responses, not carnal reactions.

Danny Silk writes, "When you have healthy boundaries, you stay in control of the resources of your life and manage them toward your priorities." The most important boundary in your life is the one that protects your secret place, your unfettered gaze at God's face and His at yours. Truly powerful people are never a victim of "the outside", the outside is a perpetual victim of their "inside" (1 John 4:4). They live by the Spirit, from the inside out.

10. Faith. Faith is trusting in God's character – that He is who He says He is, and will do what He says He will do; that His promises are true for us. In faith we can dream big. We can choose to live a life of faith that is prepared to take risks and has hope in the future. In faith we can declare impossible things that don't exist as though they do. In faith we pursue greater intimacy with our Lord, power encounters, greater revelation and miraculous interventions in our life and in the lives of those around us.

The Bible teaches that by faith alone can man enter soul rest (Hebrews 3:19; 4:3). That faith does not come from great striving, but from great surrender. Faith receives or lays hold of that which is already purchased. Faith stands on the good news: "It is finished."

Selah...

"I am out to win souls. It is my business to seek the lost. It is my business to make everyone hungry, dissatisfied, mad or glad. I want to see every person filled with the Holy Spirit. I must have a message from heaven that will not leave people as I found them. Something must happen if we are filled with the Holy Spirit. Something must happen at every place. Men must know that a man filled with the Holy Spirit is no longer a man."

–Smith Wigglesworth

"The Holy Spirit is still among us with transforming power for that one who hears the gospel message and really believes it. He still converts. He still regenerates. He still transforms."
—A.W. Tozer

DAY 26
A DEEPER SENSE OF THANKFULNESS

———•———

"One of the main reasons that we lose our enthusiasm in life
is because we become ungrateful … we let what was once
a miracle become common to us. We get so accustomed to
His goodness it becomes a routine."
—Joel Osteen

A spirit of gratitude and thankfulness is surely one of the great keys of the kingdom. The beginning of man's rebellion against God was the lack of a thankful heart. Do we genuinely desire and long for God, or for other things? The truth of the matter is, if we are not content and grateful for what we have and who we are, then we are not loving God as we should. As Francis Schaeffer put it, we are "coveting against God."

A thankless spirit wants things now. Rather than being impatient, we need to learn to love the journey we are on more than the point of arrival; to learn to embrace trust rather than control. There is a supernatural power in expressing our thanksgiving to God that brings divine multiplication. Murmuring and moaning put our focus on lack. Thanksgiving is aware of abundance.

Each day we have is a gift, not a right. Our attitude towards life, towards our God, will determine the quality of the "soil" of our life and whether God can plant seed there that will lead to an abundant harvest of blessing.

We can choose unbelief, murmuring and complaining against God, which leads to anger and anxiety. Or we can choose thankfulness, which leads to peace and rest.

Entitlement breeds envy, greed and restlessness. Gratitude

waters the garden of our heart with wonder, joy and faith. The grass is not greener next door – it's greener where we water it! Let us unwrap the gift of "today" with the childlike humility and awe that God's gift deserves.

Thankfulness results in a willingness to surrender to God's will for our lives, because we trust Him to be who He says He is for us – the perfect Father.

If we want two good indications of how much we are really trusting God, we should pay attention to our levels of anxiety and anger when things don't go our way, and to the steadiness of our stream of thanksgiving, whatever the circumstances.

"We would worry less if we praised more. Thanksgiving is the enemy of discontent and dissatisfaction." –Henry Allen Ironside.

DAY 27
TESTING TIMES

———·———

"We must cease striving and trust God to provide what He thinks is best and in whatever time He chooses to make it available. But this kind of trusting doesn't come naturally. It's a spiritual crisis of the will in which we must choose to exercise faith."
—Charles R. Swindoll

Every follower of Jesus will experience wilderness times. The wilderness exposes our appetites, our sources of trust, our obedience levels and our true place of worship. Adversity introduces a man to himself. As Israel discovered, the wilderness is humbling, hard, ordained by God, and to do us good in the end (Deuteronomy 8:14-16).

The wilderness is a vital part of our development, but it is meant for our promotion! Trials and testing force the necessary questions. *Where ultimately does my life, peace, joy and identity come from? It makes us ask ourselves: Where have I placed my trust? Is God my God or is He really my butler?*

As Jesus modelled for us, the wilderness teaches us to deal with lies, forsake idolatry, and to stand on the "it is written" of God's word. Steve Backlund quips, "God likes to send people to deserts to teach them how to repent. To change the way we think."

The wilderness testing is one that refines our character, purging all the rubbish and keeping the gold. A friend of mine, Mike, noted that, "the most powerful son of the King is he whose trust is tested and nothing changes."

I never thought I'd say it, but suffering in the wilderness

is beautiful, despite the pain and agony. Why? Because it drives us into His glorious presence. And it is here that our faith is distilled and strengthened. Out of testing comes true joy and an unshakeable trust, because we discover that our God is always with us. Suffering adds a new dimension to our spiritual life, resulting in lasting peace.

In the wilderness it's tempting to cry out, "God, get me out of here!" But often God won't change our circumstances until we relinquish our trust in them as the source of our longed-for security. He is too good and loves us too much to allow us to become victims and addicts who trust in things built on shaky foundations that can never satisfy us.

Paradoxically, as Abraham discovered, testing produces deeper trust (Romans 4:16-22). God wants us to know that, despite what is going on around us, His presence and power is within us. Our circumstances need have no bearing on the quality of our inner spiritual life and peace.

It is tempting to think that we must do something to break out of the wilderness, but trusting children wait. Unbelief leads to impulsive, sometimes reckless behaviour. In the Genesis account of the life of Joseph we read that Joseph's engineering ways with Pharaoh's chief butler arguably cost him an extra two years in prison (Genesis 40-41). Perhaps God had to purge the last bit of carnal independence from Joseph's character so as to form in him that rare, Christ-like quality of meekness. Faith believes and relies fully on God and His will to be done. Be still and wait on the Lord. Your heart will be strengthened.

The purest worship is to trust in the nature of God when our circumstances seem to bring conflict. As Brennan Manning said, "Trust is purified in the crucible of trial."

DAY 28
SHAME – THE EXIT OF THE SON

—————·—————

"Shame is the fear of disconnection – is there something about me that if other people know it or see it, that I won't be worthy of connection?"
–Brene Brown

Shame. To some extent we all live with it – a debilitating disease, the cause of identity crisis, which robs us of abundant life. No one talks about shame. And the less you talk about shame the more you have it.

The story of creation tells us that in the beginning man was created by love, to be loved, and to love back. Made in the image of God, a triune, eternal, perfectly loving relationship, human beings are wired (neuro-biologically) for connection, belonging and intimacy – with God first then each other (Genesis 2:18). Connection, love, is why we're here.

In the garden, Adam and Eve enjoyed communion, relationship and intimacy with God and each other without shame or fear. There was perfect belonging. This is God's plan. The end of Genesis chapter two reads *"They were naked and unashamed."* In other words, Adam and Eve were fully seen, fully known, happy in their own skin and there was no pretence or hiding. This community of perfect "belonging" is human paradise. And we're all after it, whether we know it or not.

Catastrophically, by Genesis chapter 3 Adam and Eve had sinned, were afraid and they hid from God and each other. The tree of life (intimacy with Jesus) was replaced with the tree of knowledge (independence, judgement and self-centredness).

To the degree that we are still hiding, and failing to manifest our true design, to that degree shame is robbing us of our true inheritance. It is also robbing the world around us who are supposed to benefit from our God-given role in His story.

Shame always looks for a protective covering. In our modern age, achievement, material possession, addictions, numbing distractions, and a search for significance apart from Christ, have replaced the fig leaves. In the following chapters we will look at how we begin to get free of shame and learn to live in God's plan of belonging and intimacy.

DAY 29
SHAME – THE RETURN OF THE SON

"Bring out the best robe and put it on him."
–The Father (Luke 15:22)

How do you see yourself? Are you worthy of the best? Shame militates against our sonship. Shame's counterfeit safety and control needs to be dismantled in our lives, so that trust and naked, unashamed sonship can take root. The antidote to shame is to relinquish control, stop pretending, and let ourselves be known and loved as we really are by the Father. The antidote to shame and every other curse is the gospel. We can trust the Father to love us perfectly, cover our nakedness, and justify our brokenness, as He always intended. We were created to be fully acceptable and comfortable in our own skin.

The Father isn't afraid of the rubbish in our lives. Quite the contrary. The moment we turn to Him, He comes running towards us, throws His arms around us, embraces and kisses us repeatedly. He takes our shame upon Himself. Shame is destroyed by His perfect, all-knowing, all-seeing, unconditional love. The Father is constantly waiting to run towards us, irrespective of how much mess we are caked in. The ring, the robe, and the party are on constant standby for our return.

When we know the Father is waiting to run to us, it's easier to turn to Him. Shame is self-centred, the fruit of the tree of the knowledge of good and evil. Shame is rooted in the lie that we need to "cover up" and perform well in order to deserve and receive God's love and affirmation. Such comparison thinking will always bring inadequacy and shame, because in our own opinion we will never measure up. Performance is the lie that we have to do something in order to be valued or valuable. The performance lie is as old as the Garden itself.

Shame partners with fear, and fear partners with control, pushing us ever further from our Father and from each other. The fruit of shame is fear of intimacy. The solution is to receive the covering robe of righteousness and justification by faith in Jesus Christ. The solution to shame is the tree of life – Jesus – He who was sent out of the city as the scapegoat and hung naked on a cross in order to take our shame. By faith we now receive His robe of righteousness. Human works are redundant.

Shame says that we are fatally flawed and must hide because of our unworthiness. Significance says that we are uniquely and beautifully made, a purposeful expression of God's creative genius in the earth. In Christ, we are enough!

DAY 30
SHAME – FROM HIDING TO BELONGING

———.———

"Face the facts of being what you are, for that is what
changes what you are."
–Soren Kierkegaard

Acceptance is the beginning of healing. Embracing who
we are and where we are at in life is what will transform
us. Remember, God loves you and me as we are, not as we
should be. If shame causes us to avoid intimacy, then moving
from shame to acceptance and belonging must involve the
following steps:

1. Intimacy and Vulnerability. Be vulnerable with God. Just
as shame causes us to hide, vulnerability lets us be seen. If
shame is the fear that our longed-for intimacy will be lost,
practicing vulnerability is moving in the opposite direction. Be
encouraged: our beauty is in being truly seen and known by
God. Therefore what makes us vulnerable makes us beautiful.
Vulnerability puts a stop to the armour of superficial
relationship and the fig leaves of performance. Vulnerability
is a form of confession and the Bible teaches that there is
deep healing in confession, humility and living in the light.
Vulnerability fuels connection and intimacy. Vulnerability
isn't comfortable, but it is necessary. God made Himself
supremely vulnerable to us in Jesus; let's follow His example.

2. Acceptance – Embrace yourself. Judgement of ourselves
and others is the potting soil of shame, whilst acceptance is
shame's enemy. Thomas Merton said, "Who am I? I am one

loved by Christ." The cross of Calvary demonstrates that we are worthy of unconditional love. We are enough. Practice self-acceptance. Practice being imperfect, unfinished, and yet completely lovable. Understanding our worthiness in Christ diffuses the power of judgement, self-hatred, perfectionism and criticism of ourselves and others. Don't apologise for being the person God made you to be. You are God's very good idea.

3. Authenticity – Be real. Embrace "stark, raving honesty" (Alcoholics Anonymous). Living authentically, from the inside out, is the enemy of shame. No more pretending, covering up; no more masks. We must be willing to let go of who we think we should be, in order to be who we really are. Someone once said that beautiful is "be-you-to-the-full."

4. Courage – Live courageously. The original definition of courage comes from "cour", meaning heart. Let's tell the story of who we are wholeheartedly.

5. Compassion – Have compassion. Jack Frost said, "You will treat others according to how you think God feels about you." Loving ourselves and others well, hearing their stories and showing kindness, casts out fear and shame. It is very difficult to be critical (of ourselves or others) when we are being compassionate.

6. Other Centred-ness – Get into community. Shame is deeply self-centred and drives us into hiding. It breeds loneliness, disconnection, narcissism and individualism. The solution is to throw ourselves into godly community and serve. We walk out our healing journey with others who will love and accept us as we are.

7. Intimacy with God – Seek Jesus, the tree of life. All shame, fear and control are swallowed up in the wonderful presence of perfect love. We must focus on Jesus and abide in His unconditional love. We are transformed by time in His presence, gazing at His face, being filled with His Spirit, and by having our mind renewed in His word (2 Corinthians 3:18, Romans 5:5, Romans 12:2).

Be God-conscious, Christ-centred and free in His Spirit.
   Be seen. Be you, uncut. Be strong. Belong. Be loved.

DAY 31
CHANGING OUR VIEW OF REPENTANCE

—·—

"Low self-esteem causes me to believe that I have so little
worth that my response does not matter. With repentance,
however, I understand that being worth so much to God is
why my response is so important."
—John Ortberg

Repentance has not been a popular message in recent times.
I see two causes: first, it has often been delivered poorly
and has a bad press, for many conjuring up images of wild-
eyed street evangelists preaching fire and brimstone without
compassion. Secondly, as Joseph Parker puts it, it can be that
"the man whose little sermon is 'repent' sets himself against
his age, and will for the time being be battered mercilessly
by the age whose moral tone he challenges. There is but one
end for such a man: 'Off with his head!' You had better not
try to preach repentance until you have pledged your head
to heaven."

But at its heart, repentance is a gracious command to
realign our thinking with God's – to know the truth and be
set free. Repentance is beautiful. It's what saves us and what
continually transforms us!

The call to repentance should never be dumbed down lest
we rob Jesus of His inheritance and the bride of Christ of her
destiny. The message of repentance will always be central
to the mission of the Church. Our privilege is to help change
the minds of others regarding Christ and so help change their
direction regarding eternity. Most importantly, without the
call to repentance, we render the cross redundant. As Paul
wrote, *"If righteousness could be achieved by the law then*

Christ died in vain." The kingdom of God is always near, but it cannot be accessed without the key of repentance.

The literal meaning of "repent" is to turn around and face in the opposite direction. At its simplest, repentance is turning away from depending on ourselves to depending entirely on Jesus and trusting in Him. Repentance is not deciding to change our behaviour (because that won't last), it's changing our minds so that God's grace can work in us and, in due course, our behaviour will follow suit.

"Repent" was the first message preached by John the Baptist, Jesus, and Peter because God in His compassion was appealing to all those who were "facing the wrong way", heading towards darkness instead of the light.

The message of repentance is one of saving compassion, not condemnation. Father God seeks to draw us, by His love, to embrace His Son, Jesus, and trust in Him alone. The cross of Christ remains an offence to many – because people don't like to be confronted with their sin, nor be reminded that their self-righteous deeds will never justify them before God. But if we live in a state of grace-fuelled repentance (daily having our minds renewed), we will find that our lives are transformed to bear much spiritual fruit. Repentance often requires some distress and pain for it to be lasting. Paul wrote that he was *"not sorry that I sent that severe letter to you ... I am glad I sent it, not because it hurt you, but because the pain caused you to repent and change your ways ... For godly sorrow produces repentance **leading** to salvation"* (2 Corinthians 7:8-10).

Jesus said, *"Whoever sins is a slave to sin"* (John 8:34) and so a slave to suffering. The kindness of God leads to the majestic outcome of repentance.

DAY 32
LOSING OURSELVES

———•———

"God's means of delivering us from sin is not by making us stronger and stronger, but by making us weaker and weaker. That is surely rather a peculiar way of victory, you say; but it is the divine way. God sets us free from the dominion of sin, not by strengthening our old man but by crucifying him; not by helping him to do anything, but by removing him from the scene of action."
—Watchman Nee

Eugene Peterson said that the essence of the spiritual life is "learning how to die". "You start losing all your illusions, and you start being capable of true intimacy and love."

We have a problem. We want to have a vibrant spiritual life with all of God's blessings ... we just don't want to get there "by way of death", as Augustine said. Father Raniero was asked by Nicky Gumbel, "How do you grow in your walk with Christ?" He responded, "The ego must die, for Christ to live." Paul wrote, *"I die daily"* (1 Corinthians 15:31) and *"those who are Christ's have crucified the flesh with its passions and desires"* (Galatians 5:24).

How do you know if your ego is not dead? Have a look at how you respond to trouble. Dan Mohler has said that if we can't "glory in tribulation" and see the "manifestation of Jesus" in our troubles, then a self-centred, self-pitying force is at work. We cry out, "Why me?" Here we must go back to the secret place with the Father and die to that self-centred thing. It's not what we are going through that matters, it's what God is doing in our life at that point that is important. When our ego is put to death, the life of the resurrected Christ can flow out of us.

Dying to self is another unpopular message in our culture of entitlement! Most people want to be happy, but their self-focused pursuit of happiness is fatally flawed. Happiness is only ever a bi-product of seeking something else. True, lasting happiness is a result of dethroning ourselves and seeking first Christ and His kingdom.

The Bible doesn't teach us that "Blessed is the one who seeks blessedness." It comes as we prioritise God and His kingdom over our comfort. Paraphrasing Jesus in the Sermon on the Mount, "The person who will find happiness is the one who stops trying so hard to be happy." Without the singular focus of Christ in our lives we will be tempted to put our trust in many other things and the peace of God will elude us.

C.S. Lewis wrote, "There must be a real giving up of the self. You must throw it away blindly, so to speak ... Give up your self, and you will find your real self. Lose your life and you will save it. Submit to death, the death of your ambitions and favourite wishes every day, and death of your whole body in the end ... submit with every fibre of your being, and you will find eternal life. Keep back nothing."

Read and reflect on the challenging words of George Müller: "There was a day when I died; died to self, my opinions, preferences, tastes and will; died to the world, its approval or censure; died to the approval or blame even of my brethren or friends; and since then I have studied only to show myself approved unto God."

DAY 33
TRUE HOPE

—•—

"The word *hope* I take for *faith*; and indeed hope is nothing
else but the constancy of faith."
—John Calvin

Hope is like the oxygen of life. The Bible says that when
hope is deferred or taken away, it makes the heart sick
(Proverbs 13:12). A lack of hope may lead to discouragement,
confusion, disillusionment, bitterness, cynicism and more.
Hope, however, is one of Father God's greatest gifts to His
children. We are purveyors of the only great hope!

Steve Backlund says, "My hope level is the indicator of
whether I am believing lies or truth. The more hope you have
the more truth you are believing. The less hope you have the
more lies you are believing. So hopelessness is the indicator
that we have bad beliefs in that area. The moment we believe
truth is the moment we get filled with the God of hope."

As Paul wrote, *"May the God of hope fill you with all joy
and peace as you trust in him, so that you may overflow with
hope by the power of the Holy Spirit"* (Romans 15:13).

Our hope level is dependent on our belief system. If there
is an area of our life in which we have no hope, then we have
believed a lie. The fruit of believing lies about ourselves is
despair. As Jeremy Taylor said, "It is impossible for that man
to despair who remembers that his Helper is omnipotent."

Similarly, John Piper wrote, "All things are possible with
God! In front the words give hope and behind they give
humility. They are the antidote to despair and pride."

What then is hope? True hope is resting in the knowledge

that we have a loving Father who holds every single aspect of our life in His hands; a Father who is completely committed to caring for us and providing for us as His child. When things happen in life to unsettle us, the enemy would like us to fall into despair – because that undermines our belief in the constancy and consistency of God. The enemy would like us to believe either that sometimes God is absent, or that He has changed His mind. Neither is true!

When we have faith and continue to trust in Him, we will find, as T.D. Jakes said, that "God's grace is painted on the canvas of despair."

Selah...

"You can chase after all the pleasures and philosophies of the world, but your spirit is not interested in them. Your spirit just wants God."
—Derek Prince

"The flesh always values something more than Christ ... But the Spirit points to richer treasure. He always holds up Christ. The battle between competing affections defines the war between the flesh and the Spirit. Which treasure will be our first place passion? What do we value most?"
—Larry Crabb

DAY 34
REALITY CHECK

———•———

"A prepared heart is better than a prepared sermon."
—E.M. Bounds

If we want to reach others for Christ then we need to realise that our hearts are our sermons. We preach our lives. That is why it is so important that our faith is grounded and real; that our lives are lived with transparency.

Our "ministry" as believers is no more significant in the church or the workplace than it is at the breakfast table or the corner shop. It begins and ends with the quality of our heart. As the scripture says, *"Keep your heart with all diligence, for out of it spring the issues of life."* (Proverbs 4:23)

In Greek culture a "hypocrite" was an actor who wore various masks. If we are constantly wearing masks and pretending to be something we're not, then we're hypocrites too! If ever we are transparent we call it a virtue, but actually it should be our base camp in life, our starting point. Ultimately, God will not judge us on our works, but on our heart motivation. We need to ask ourselves in any given circumstance, "Am I acting like a person after God's heart?"

A "prepared heart" seeks not to gain but to give away. Jesus counselled His disciples to beware of covetousness (Luke 12:15) – which is an impatient and lustful desire to acquire. The world covets, but we are to live to give our lives away for the sake of the Kingdom. If we want to gain our life in Christ, then we are to lose it; to give it away. Children of God are not possessive or territorial, because all that the Father has is theirs. There is always more than enough to go around.

While others may look at outward circumstances and see the sum total of their lives, our lives are lived from the inside out. God is working on our heart foundations, establishing our faith and making us secure. His ways are higher. As we follow Him He leads us into greater realms of freedom and glory.

How we react to others speaks of our inner life. Relational tests come to us most days. The wealth of our hearts will dictate whether we are lean, insecure, proud and take offence, or generous, humble, and rooted in the Father's love, extending grace. Our fruit always reveals our roots. The need to be right flows out of a poverty of heart. A royal spirit has no need for vindication, will demonstrate meekness and is able to forgive debts and move on. Dan Mohler commented, "If I am squeezed, Christ should manifest."

Let's live and love out of hearts filled with God's grace. Pray now and ask your loving Father to heal any hurts and adjust any attitudes in your life where you need to reflect Him more. He is gracious and kind.

DAY 35
BE FILLED AND TAKE POSSESSION

"To this end I also labour, striving according to His working which works in me mightily."
(Colossians 1:29)

Our God-given vocation and mission in life is fuelled by the fire of God. Reinhard Bonnke commented, "The less Holy Spirit we have, the more cake and coffee we need to keep the church going." We must become Holy Spirit addicts! (Acts 2:3-4, Ephesians 5:18). It is our sole responsibility to be intimate with Him, so that He can fuel the Kingdom purpose He has deposited within us. If we stay fuelled up, neither man nor the devil will prevail against us.

As believers, we need to be aware of our inheritance and calling. We need to know our territory and possess it, saying with confidence, "It's mine." There are too many nice Christians around. Stop being so nice and get spiritually possessive!

Sons know their Father, know their enemy, and know their mandate. Our mission is to take spiritual ground and win back territory for the kingdom. Our enemy is simply waiting to be conquered, already defeated by the cross of Christ.

We need to stop putting imaginary limits on ourselves and on God. His power knows no bounds, and when we are walking in our purpose, trusting in the power of God, we are literally unstoppable.

Our enemy likes to get us confused about our purpose. He will weary us with distractions. But take heart, because God is with us and for us! John Wesley (in a letter to William

Wilberforce) wrote,

"Unless God has raised you up for this very thing, you will be worn out by the opposition of men and devils. But if God be for you, who can be against you? Are all of them together stronger than God? O, be not weary of well doing!"

Eugene Peterson has written that, "The mature Christian life involves a congruence of grace and work." Without grace we are both powerless and fruitless.

We grow in grace through intimacy with our Father and then, through grace, we work according to His purpose. Grace disarms striving, but empowers diligence. Without gracious diligence we will not inherit God's promises for our life. Inheritance requires co-labouring with the Father. Press on with "spiritual violence" in faith and lay hold of all that Jesus died for – empowered by the grace of God!

(Read and reflect on Hebrews 6:10-12; Matthew 11:12; Ephesians 2:8-10; Philippians 3:12-14).

DAY 36
THE SECRET OF THE FATHER'S DISCIPLINE

———•———

"For whom the Lord loves He chastens, and scourges every
son whom He receives."
(Hebrews 12:6)

RT Kendall writes, "In August 1956 I fell across the bed in my grandmother's house in near despair. I cried out, 'Why?' Everything seemed to have gone wrong and the future was bleak. In Hebrews the word we are dealing with comes from the verb *paideo* – to discipline. The meaning of the word in this verse is 'enforced learning'. Chastening, or being disciplined, is essentially preparation. It is not God getting even, but getting us ready. In a word: He chastens us because He is not finished with us yet." (From *Pure Joy*)

Those who have chosen to follow the path of unrighteousness are left alone by God to pursue their own ends. The last thing we want is to be left alone by God. Discipline in the Refiner's fire is, to the believer, not a sign of God's cruelty but of His care. It is loving, wise attention from a perfect Father who is fashioning us after the image of His Son. As John Arnott says, "God loves us just as we are, but He loves us too much to leave us where we are at." We all go through trials in life – let's not waste them! We must guard our hearts with diligence and count it joy when God allows the circumstances of our lives to shape us. It is just our Father further embellishing the masterpiece He's working on.

As A.W. Tozer poignantly put it, "It is doubtful whether God can bless a man greatly until He has hurt him deeply." Charles Spurgeon unpacks the subject further: "I bear willing witness that I owe more to the fire, the hammer and the file than to anything else in the Lord's workshop. I sometimes question whether I have ever learned anything except through the rod. When my schoolroom is darkened, I see the most."

Or, as renowned theologian A.W. Pink once put it, "Chastisement is designed for our good, to promote our highest interests. Look beyond the rod to the all-wise hand that wields it."

As believers, we may experience a lot of affliction in life. And some of it is our own doing! It is never pleasant. Whatever the cause, we need to know that if we stay humble, our perfect Father weaves His merciful, gracious, redemptive hand in the midst of it all, bringing beauty out of ashes. God is so good – He takes no pleasure whatsoever in our afflictions – but He is wise enough to allow them if, as Andrew Murray put it, "He can thereby guide His beloved child to come home and abide in the beloved Son."

I love the blessings of being a child of God. I am thrilled to know and live in the truth that His goodness and mercy chase me down every day, particularly when I make a mess of things. And I'm not a fan of pain. But I fear that the modern Church has lost its theology of "chastisement", opting for comfort and preferring to speak disproportionately about external winning and succeeding – as if any sort of affliction meant that we have somehow failed to appropriate all of God's blessings.

The power and purpose of suffering will return when we focus intently on the cross and rightly acknowledge His command to pick up ours daily (Luke 14:27). Without the dimension of suffering we are a shallow, fleshly bride, with less capacity for joy. The suffering of chastisement should not cause us to question our sonship; rather it legitimises it and lends it eternal, hope-filled purpose.

(Meditate on Hebrews 12:5-11)

DAY 37
LIMITLESS GRACE

———•———

"What gives me the most hope every day is God's grace; knowing that His grace is going to give me the strength for whatever I face; knowing that nothing is a surprise to God."
—Rick Warren

The Christian life is grace from beginning to end. The realm in which we now live is entirely different. It has nothing to do with our former, unregenerate way of life. Consequently, all our thinking as a Christian must be different. Religion thrives on trying to earn the underserved and purchase righteousness. As a result, religion makes us feel proud when we succeed and guilty when we don't. It makes us unmerciful and judgmental towards those who don't make the mark. Grace, however, outrageously gives us what we don't deserve.

But we must always remember that the grace of Jesus Christ is a costly grace. As Dietrich Bonhoeffer writes: "Cheap grace is the preaching of forgiveness without requiring repentance, baptism without church discipline, communion without confession, absolution without personal confession. Cheap grace is grace without discipleship, grace without the cross, grace without Jesus Christ, living and incarnate."

He goes on to say that costly grace is surrendering to the kingly rule of Christ. Costly, because it calls us to abandon our selfish plans and desires to follow Jesus. "Costly" because it costs us our lives, and "grace" because it justifies sinners. We have been bought by God for a very high price.

Reflect on the following truths about God's incredible gift:

1. God's grace is abundant. It's scandalous because it gives us freely what we can never possibly deserve or earn.

2. God's grace is sufficient. God's grace to us is a bottomless pit, a fountain that never runs dry.

3. God's grace makes us bold. When we understand God's limitless grace we can pray big prayers. We can plan big things and be audacious in our faith. We can cry out, "I'm your son – I'm not letting go until you bless me!"

4. God's grace makes us gracious. The critical and the fearful don't understand grace. The gospel is good news for bad people and bad news for good people!

"My friends, if this is not good news to you, you have never understood the gospel of grace." (Brennan Manning, *The Ragamuffin Gospel*)

DAY 38
A MEDITATION ON LOVE

———•———

"And now these three remain: faith, hope and love. But the greatest of these is love."

(1 Corinthians 13:13)

Smith Wigglesworth said, "Perfect love will never want the pre-eminence in everything, it will never want to take the place of another, it will always be willing to take the back seat."

Today, think about this meditation on love:

Love has many different flavours. As well as being patient and kind it can be righteously angry, yet it is not easily provoked to anger.

Love becomes most real when we show it to someone who dislikes us or disagrees with us, for love has to be tested.

Love speaks the truth, even when the truth is politically incorrect, and love prays.

Love burns for the lost, cares not for worldly reputation, and takes risks to the point of death. Love dies daily to release resurrection power.

Love prefers to give rather than receive. Love is crazy generous! Love prefers others. Love serves whilst remaining childlike and full of joy.

Love is a choice, then an action.

Love looks and sees the gold in others; sees the end of their race, not their past or present struggles.

Love is grateful and humble. Love always encourages.

Love isn't anxious or worried, but trusts.

Love is sometimes like a raging fire and sometimes like a lamb, silent before its executioner.

Love meets us where we are, but is too kind to leave us there.

DAY 39
CHOSEN ONES

—•—

"In Him you also trusted, after you heard the word of truth,
the gospel of your salvation; in whom also, having believed,
you were sealed with the Holy Spirit of promise, who is the
guarantee of our inheritance until the redemption of the
purchased possession, to the praise of His glory."
(Ephesians 1:13-14)

Orphan-hood is a global epidemic – the separation of man from the love of God. The Bible makes it clear that every person is born an orphan because of the Fall. We are all initially cut off from experiencing God's loving presence, but the Father is working to gather us back to Himself. Our enemy is working to try to prevent us from discovering God's father heart. John Eldridge writes,

"This is the enemy's one central purpose – to separate us from the Father. He uses neglect to whisper, 'You see – no one cares. You're not worth caring about.' He uses a sudden loss of innocence to whisper, 'This is a dangerous world, and you are alone. You've been abandoned'... And in this way he makes it nearly impossible for us to know what Jesus knew, makes it so very, very hard to come to the Father's heart towards us." (John Eldridge, *Fathered by God*)

Jesus, through His death on the cross – the ultimate representation of God's love for us – has made a way back to the Father. Jesus came to reveal to us the true nature of the Father. Through Jesus, God has adopted us and restored us back to His family. It is here, as an adopted son or daughter, that we finally discover who we really are; who we are meant to be. As Henri Nouwen writes,

"You must hold on to the truth that you are the chosen one. That truth is the bedrock on which you can build a life as the Beloved. When you lose touch with your chosenness, you expose yourself to the temptation of self-rejection, and that temptation undermines the possibility of ever growing as the Beloved." (extract from *Life of the Beloved*).

Sometimes, in our brokenness, it is hard to understand that we are the beloved of God the Father, but the truth is, we have been chosen. Nouwen continues,

"God's love is a love that includes all people – each one in his or her uniqueness. It is only when we have claimed our own place in God's love that we can experience this all-embracing, non-comparing love and feel safe, not only with God, but also with all our brothers and sisters..."

Reflect on this truth today:

"You received the Spirit of adoption by whom we cry out, 'Abba, Father.' The Spirit Himself bears witness with our spirit that we are children of God." (Romans 8:15-16)

DAY 40
ALL IS GRACE

———.———

"But by the grace of God I am what I am, and his grace to me was not without effect. No, I worked harder than all of them—yet not I, but the grace of God that was with me."
(1 Corinthians 15:10)

Milton Jones said that, "If being a Christian is just about trying to be like Jesus on your own, you might as well be an Elvis impersonator!"

Jesus said, *"Blessed are the poor in spirit, for theirs is the kingdom of heaven"* (Matthew 5:3). Being "poor in spirit" describes a state of humility where we realise that everything comes to us simply as a gift of grace. As Bill Johnson says, "Nothing is deserved, even on my best day. Even some outrageous display of faith – even that was a gift from God."

Reflect on this meditation on grace...

- Grace is getting what you don't deserve
- Grace is giving what isn't deserved
- Grace is the gift of life
- Grace is that everything good is a gift from God
- Grace is that every breath breathed is a gift
- Grace is that we are His creation and we are not our own
- Grace is that we are made for His glory
- Grace is unconditional love – a love that is constant whether we are sinning or doing good works
- Grace is that there is nothing I can do to make God love me more and nothing I can do to make Him love me less
- Grace is everlasting mercy and forgiveness

- Grace is that everything good is from God who reigns
- Grace covers sin and overlooks offence
- Grace is that He did it all to redeem us and continues to do it all; without Him we can do nothing of any eternal value
- Grace is God as a man, executed naked on a tree by His creation in order to redeem us

Selah...

"'Wait on the Lord' is a constant refrain in the Psalms, and it is a necessary word, for God often keeps us waiting. He is not in such a hurry as we are, and it is not His way to give more light on the future than we need for action in the present, or to guide us more than one step at a time. When in doubt, do nothing, but continue to wait on God. When action is needed, light will come."
—J.I. Packer

DAY 41
IDENTITY AND AUTHORITY

———·———

"Just as you know how we were exhorting and encouraging and imploring each one of you as a father would his own children."

(1 Thessalonians 2:11)

It is when we receive the revelation that we are God's children that we understand our true kingdom identity. Before we can really move on in God, we need to find our identity as children of the Most High, the Creator of Heaven and Earth. Out of that identity we will understand what He has called us to do and receive what we need to accomplish the task.

As Bill Johnson has said, "The devil and God are asking you the same question: 'Who do you think you are?' You either live from your identity or you live for your identity."

We need to come before our Heavenly Father and ask Him to show us how He sees us. As the Holy Spirit ministers to us, God will pinpoint any ungodly beliefs we hold about ourselves, and will help us replace them with godly beliefs as He shows us how He perceives us.

You are the son/daughter of the King of kings, so learn to live life king-size!

Mark Stibbe writes, "The greater the revelation of your kingdom identity, the greater the release of your kingdom authority. You need the robe and the ring."

Once we are secure in our "sonship" we are ready to be groomed as spiritual fathers and mothers in the faith. Becoming a spiritual father/mother means that, like Jesus, we need to "look like" the Father.

God is a loving Father, so as we become more and more like Him, this new role unfolds and we are ready to nurture others, to love in greater depth, and to help others to discover and embrace their kingdom identity and mandate.

Just as Jesus revealed the nature of the Father to us, it is our job to reveal the nature of God to those around us through love and acceptance. But we must have love-encounters first, to experience that love for ourselves, to grasp the vastness of this love. Like Paul, let's make it our aim in life to be imitators of God – an example to all believers.

"Therefore be imitators of God as dear children. And walk in love, as Christ also has loved us and given Himself for us, an offering and a sacrifice to God for a sweet-smelling aroma." (Ephesians 5:1-2)

DAY 42
CRAZY FOR GOD

In the fourteenth century John Wycliffe stood against the tyranny of religious greed, fear, control and heresy by writing the first English translation of the Bible and putting it in the hands of the common man. He also trained up a band of preachers that travelled town-to-town across the UK proclaiming the gospel and winning the lost. Wycliffe obeyed the Great Commission and paved the way for the reformation. Now it is our time.

Today God wants to kick the church out of the church! When we read about Jesus and the early apostles we see they were almost never in a formal church meeting. Christianity is not about church attendance, it is about becoming like Christ. The early apostles were church, full time – His body, His hands and feet, His mouth proclaiming the gospel, touching the sick, driving out demons and raising dead people. It was messy, dangerous and glorious, and it all played out among the people on the streets as the kingdom of God crashed in supernaturally, "turning the world upside down" (Acts 17:6).

The Great Commission hasn't changed, but today it takes holy rebellion to swim against the tide of stuffy, pew-warming religion and be about the Lord's business in the chaotic, perishing sea of humanity. The Church is not as a pleasure cruiser but a lifeboat. Dr Vance Havner writes,

"It is not our business to make the message acceptable, but to make it available. We are not to see that they like it, but that they get it."

I was at a drinks party the other evening, chatting to a lovely Christian couple when the man piped up enthusiastically,

"Oh, you're that crazy street preacher aren't you?"

"Arguably," I replied, rather dryly.

It's interesting to me that in the Church we are quick to label something commanded multiple times by Jesus as "crazy", rather than, for example, "faithful" or "obedient". The man was kind and certainly not intending to be unhelpful, but it gave me pause for thought. I believe it's time for "crazy" to become "normal"!

One day our whole lives will be evaluated and measured by the weight of our faithfulness to Jesus Christ and our love for souls. Dr W.E. Sangster has a sobering thought: "How shall I feel at the judgment, if multitudes of missed opportunities pass before me ... and all my excuses prove to be disguises of my cowardice and pride?"

Finally, meditate upon this thought from Leonard Ravenhill: "Could a mariner sit idle if he heard the drowning cry? Could a doctor sit in comfort and just let his patients die? Could a fireman sit idle, let men burn and give no hand? Can you sit at ease in Zion with the world around you damned?"

Lord, grant us boldness to share your message.

DAY 43
THE NAME

——·——

"What we believe about healing is
rooted in our image of God."
–Randy Clark

Names reveal a lot about a person. The following names of God reveal different aspects of His nature and paint a vivid picture of what He is like. Elohim is the first name for God found in the Bible, meaning strength or power and is a plural form. Elohim is combined with other words to describe different characteristics of our Father:

- *Elohay Kedem* – God of the Beginning (Deuteronomy 33:27)
- *Elohay Mishpat* – God of Justice (Isaiah 30:18)
- *Elohay Selichot* – God of Forgiveness (Nehemiah 9:17)
- *Elohay Mikarov* – God Who is Near (Jeremiah 23:23)
- *Elohay Elohim* – God of Gods (Deuteronomy 10:17)
- *Elohim Kedoshim* – Holy God (Leviticus 19:2, Joshua 24:19)
- *Elohim Chaiyim* – Living God (Jeremiah 10:10)

YHVH is the special name for God (meaning "to be") that we render, Jehovah. Again, combined with other words it reveals more of God's character to us:

- *Jehovah Nissi* – the Lord my Banner or the Lord my Miracle (Exodus 17:15)
- *Jehovah Raah* – the Lord my Shepherd (which can be translated "the Lord my Friend") (Psalm 23)
- *Jehovah Rapha* – the Lord that Heals (Exodus 15:26)

- *Jehovah Jireh* – the Lord Will Provide (Genesis 22:14)
- *Jehovah Shalom* – the Lord is Peace (Judges 6:24)

In the New Covenant Jesus has become the ultimate revelation of God – perfect theology (John 10:30). The writer of Hebrews puts it like this: *"He is the sole expression of the glory of God [the Light-being, the out-raying or radiance of the divine], and He is the perfect imprint and very image of [God's] nature"* (Hebrews 1:1-3). Jesus unveiled one aspect of God that, until He came, no one had been aware of. He revealed God as a loving, intimate, relational Father – Abba – "Daddy". What does Scripture say about this heavenly Daddy who is our Father? Meditate on the following truths:

- My heavenly Daddy is perfect (Matthew 5:48)
- My heavenly Daddy's only motivation towards me is love (John 17:23, 26)
- My heavenly Daddy is only and always good (Matthew 19:17, James 1:17)
- My heavenly Daddy is joyful, peaceful, longsuffering, kind, gentle and self-controlled (Galatians 5:22-23)
- My heavenly Daddy is faithful and will never leave me (1 Corinthians 10:13, Romans 8:38-39)
- My heavenly Daddy will supply all my needs (Philippians 4:19)
- My heavenly Daddy doesn't want me to be alone (Genesis 2:18)
- My heavenly Daddy enables me to do all things (Philippians 4:13)
- My heavenly Daddy reigns absolutely (Psalm 97:1, Job 25:2)

- My heavenly Daddy is all powerful (Matthew 19:26)
- My heavenly Daddy is all knowing (1 John 3:20)
- My heavenly Daddy has dreamt up, with extreme creativity, flare and joy, a good, prosperous and pre-ordained plan for my unique life (Hebrews 4:3, Psalm 139:13-16, Acts 17:26,1 Thessalonians 5:24, 2 Timothy 1:9, Jeremiah 29:11)
- My heavenly Daddy's Word is the only Truth and anything that doesn't conform to it is a lie (John 14:6, John 17:17)

"It is not great men who change the world, but weak men in the hands of a great God."
—Brother Yun, *The Heavenly Man*

DAY 44
LOVE VERSUS FEAR

—•—

"God gave us a spirit not of fear but of power and love and self-control."
(2 Timothy 1:7 ESV)

Love and fear are two of the most basic drivers of human beings and we can live out of one or the other. The way of Christ is the way of love. "He who fears has not been perfected in love" writes John, the beloved apostle (1 John 4:18). That is to say, it is possible to walk in love, without a trace of fear. This is Christian perfection, where Jesus desires to take us, to become like Him. At a Washington for Jesus rally an African American Bishop commented, "If you Christians ever get over your fear, you're going to be dangerous." The command "Do not fear" appears in the Bible over three hundred times! Safe to say, God wants us to be consumed by love, not driven by fear.

The apostle Paul tells us that anything we do as believers, however heroic or astonishing, must come from a place of love, otherwise it means nothing. The battle between love and fear is a big deal, and worth fighting for. God is love (1 John 4:16). That means He has no fear, no insecurity, no self-interest, no control or rejection issues, and He isn't ashamed. And we are made in His image. To become full of His love is to become who we were always meant to be – completely free.

What an inheritance! Take some time to mediate on the following truths about love and fear:

- Fear wants to control. Love trusts and lets go
- God doesn't control anyone. He gives us complete freedom He loves and blesses those who care nothing for Him. Love never controls, but always sets free
- Thomas Merton said, "The beginning of love is the will to let those we love be perfectly themselves, the resolution not to twist them to fit our own image."
- Fear builds walls and creates distance – the opposite of intimacy
- Fear breeds in the absence of love. Love casts out fear. Intimacy (being seen by God) drives out shame
- Fearful people are likely to show you their worst. People who feel loved will show you their best
- Love is not defensive because there is no fear in love (1 John 4)
- Love celebrates what God has created. Love is happy in its own skin
- Fear is faith in the wrong kingdom
- Fear = Suspicion; Love = Trust
- Fearful people tend to dominate others and need others to make them look good. The most powerful people are rooted in love; they empower and serve others
- Fearful people are concerned with survival, so put themselves first. Love-centred people live from a place of abundance, so can put others first

DAY 45
TRUE FEAR

———•———

"We must fear God out of love, not love Him out of fear."
–Saint Francis de Sales

In today's 21st century consumer culture the "fear of God" seems antiquated and irrelevant to many, even in the Church. This is largely because it has been deeply misunderstood and perhaps delivered from a wrong heart. However, we will only grow as a body of believers when we both love God more intimately and fear Him more reverently. "Fear and love are best in conjunction," writes Thomas Watson. "Love is the sails to speed the soul's motion; and fear is the ballast to keep it steady in religion." Watson also notes that fear "keeps the heart serene" and "free from presumption".

The fear of God is not fear as the world knows it. It is entirely different in nature to unsanctified, demonically-inspired fear. True fear of the Lord is for our good. First of all it silences every other fear. Oswald Chambers writes, "The remarkable thing about fearing God is that when you fear God you fear nothing else, whereas if you do not fear God you fear everything else." Second, it doesn't drive us away from God, but draws us to Him. The fear of the Lord is a holy fear, a holy reverence, because God is an Almighty and awesome God.

When I worked in the media, there were certain film directors I worked for in London that I "feared". I revered them and I cared what they thought of me. I behaved in ways I hoped would please them. This is the fear of man. It causes us to make idols and dramatically limits our freedom and integrity to be ourselves.

In the gospel of John it says that Jesus did not *"entrust Himself"* to man, nor to *"man's testimony ... for he knew what was in a man"* (John 2:24-25). Instead, we read, *"the fear of the Lord is His treasure"* (Isaiah 33:6) and *"His delight"* (Isaiah 11:3). The fear of God frees us from the slavery of the fear of man.

Furthermore, the fear of God brings life and satisfaction (Proverbs 19:23). It brings victory against temptation (Proverbs 16:6). It leads to freedom and joyful obedience (Jeremiah 32:39-40). The fear of the Lord is a good gift from a good Father. Solomon summed up the essence of life with these words:

"Let us hear the conclusion of the whole matter: fear God and keep His commandments, For this is man's all." (Ecclesiastes 12:13)

DAY 46
FIRST THINGS FIRST

———•———

"We ought to see the face of God every morning before we
see the face of man."
–D.L. Moody

Busyness is the enemy of intimacy. Intimacy is about
attentiveness, being still and present. We are made for
intimacy. When we say "yes" to something or someone we are
saying "no" to something/someone else. When we close the
door on one invitation we are accepting another. Ultimately,
it is not what we say but our diaries that reveal our priorities!

We must beware the temptation to live busy lives through
a fear of missing out. It's so easy to be busy and distracted
that we must be ruthless about setting aside time for intimacy
with our Father. The most important boundary in our lives is
the one that protects our secret place with God.

If we don't miss or long for God's presence then we need
to ask ourselves some tough questions. Fundamentally, the
romance goes when we give our attention to other lovers,
instead of our true love. Happy are those who are hungry for
God's presence, because they will be fully satisfied. We were
created for intimacy, so maybe we should scrap our carefully
crafted prayer lists and focus on divine hunger. All our other
needs are peripheral.

Jesus put it plainly: *"Seek first the kingdom of God and His
righteousness and everything needed will be added to you"*
(Matthew 6:33). The word "first" is key. What we seek first
will affect everything that comes after it. As we seek God
first, our needs will change because we will be transformed

by God's presence. Our priorities will alter as we embark on this life-surrendering pilgrimage. Everything that comes second will become grace-endowed as we seek the Father. As William Law writes, "If you have not chosen the Kingdom of God first, it will in the end make no difference what you have chosen instead."

Judas was offended by Mary wasting a year's worth of earnings by anointing Jesus' body for burial. Restless orphans will always be offended when relationship with Jesus takes priority over doing things for Him. Focusing on "doing" rather than "being" results in self-justification. I know this place of bondage only too well. The truth is, lovers of God get more done than workers.

Swim against the tide of distraction. Shun the counterfeits of busyness and achievement. Stop and be still. Fruitfulness flows from intimacy. If we don't "waste" time with Jesus first, then we are likely to waste the rest of our time.

Selah

"I know of no other way to triumph over sin long-term than to gain a distaste for it because of a superior satisfaction in God."
–John Piper, Desiring God

"The only people who 'get better' are people who know that, if they never get better, God will love them anyway! The corollary to that principle is this: God will not only love you if you don't get better, He will teach you that 'getting better is not the issue' – His love is the issue!"
–Steve Brown

"God loves you as you are and not as you should be."
–Brennan Manning

DAY 47
THE INHERITANCE

———•———

"But the story we're given is a God-story, not an Abraham-story. What we read in scripture is, 'Abraham entered into what God was doing for him, and that was the turning point. He trusted God to set him right instead of trying to be right on his own.' … But if you see the job is too big for you, that it's only something God can do, and you trust him to do it – well, that trusting-him-to-do-it is what gets you set right with God, by God. Sheer gift."
(Romans 4:1-5 MSG)

When we become a follower of Jesus, that is the moment we leave behind our story and enter His-story. We leave behind the vanity of independent, orphan hearted-striving and embrace the abundant life of grace working through faith.

The grace of sonship takes the pressure off. God is back at the centre of things. Gracelessness puts man at the centre, makes man the initiator, man the builder and man the sustainer. Welcome to the hellish trinity of pressure, performance and perfectionism in order to "measure up" and keep life going.

The orphan lifestyle is exhausting. Whatever we build independently of God we have to try to sustain without His help.

"Unless the Lord builds the house, they labour in vain who build it." (Psalm 127:1)

With God at the centre of our life, grace is restored and only God can take the credit for the fruit and success in our lives. Living within the *"unforced rhythms of grace"* (Matthew

11:28-30 MSG) is about lying back in the arms of the Father, yielding to His divine purpose and mighty force in us, then co-labouring with Him from that place of rest. Daring to embrace what the Father wants to do in us is the best thing we can do for Him.

The more I learn about grace, the more I learn the importance of allowing. Yielding. Being. Waiting. Simply making space.

Dare to take your hands off the reigns and let the Father work with you and through you. Come as you are, go as He is. It's restful when God gets all the glory. Welcome to the life of gracious inheritance.

DAY 48
THE BEAUTY OF MEEKNESS

—·—

"The impression of Jesus which the Gospels give is not
so much one of deity reduced as of divine capacities
restrained."

–J.I. Packer

In the Sermon on the Mount Jesus famously says, *"Blessed are the meek, for they shall inherit the earth"* (Matthew 5:5). In the Passion translation it reads, *"What contentment floods you when gentleness lives in you! For you will inherit the earth."*

"Meekness" is much misunderstood and therefore the word hardly used as a result. Perhaps that explains why it is a virtue so seldom practised? Meekness is not weakness as some might suppose. The best definition is power restrained or strength under control. The Aramaic word makeekheh implies being both gentle and flexible.

Picture this, if you can: the gentle Almighty; the meek All-powerful. It fascinates me, ruins me and draws me deeper into God's heart. There is something dazzling about His gentleness. Gentleness opens people's hearts (Galatians 6).

We are at our most free in meekness, knowing that the only person we need to control is ourselves. Jesus is saying that when we claim nothing as ours, everything will be given to us. The exhaustion of vain, independent living is over.

Meekness means we can end all pretence. We can live humbly and happily knowing we are no better and no worse than the next person. When we are meek we live graciously down-to-earth, because our security and contentment is found only in God's presence. Yielded and submitted to God, our all-sufficient provider, we can live open-handedly, happy to receive and likewise to scatter.

Meekness is the language of letting go and letting God. We no longer have to live like orphans, fighting to protect ourselves, we can live like sons/daughters, losing our lives in Jesus only to find them. His yoke is easy and restful as we forsake striving. We own nothing but possess everything.

"Blessed [inwardly peaceful, spiritually secure, worthy of respect] are the gentle [the kind-hearted, the sweet-spirited, the self-controlled], for they will inherit the earth." (Matthew 5:5 AMP)

When we are meek we are beautiful, ultimately powerful and free. The truly meek can be trusted with the earth because they are channels of God.

DAY 49
JUSTIFIED

———·———

Justification is the quest of humanity. Everyone is trying to justify their existence. It is an inbuilt desire. But any justification other than that which comes through the cross of Christ is counterfeit and will lead to either pride or misery – when it is stripped away.

Yet we are all about this business of trying to justify ourselves. Like Cain, we try to please God with our efforts and sacrifices. Looking back over my life, it's tragic how often I have tried to validate my existence to both God and man through achievements. I am encouraged when I remember that although Israel left Egypt in a matter of days, it took years to get Egypt out of Israel as the people laboured under a slave mentality.

The fact that we are dependent upon the grace of God renders all self-justification worthless. Paul writes,

"Where is boasting then? It is excluded. By what law? Of works? No, but by the law of faith. Therefore we conclude that a man is justified by faith apart from the deeds of the law." (Romans 3:27-28)

Jesus says to us, *"Unless a man forsakes all he cannot be My disciple"* (Luke 14:33). In other words, until we have put into perspective material wealth, career prestige, reputation, achievement, even our own moral/religious performance, we are clinging to something other than Christ to justify our existence. Those things will puff us up when they go according to plan, and kills us when they fail. Either way the pressure is on us – we are trying to save ourselves!

Dietrich Bonhoeffer writes, "The only man who has the

right to say that he is justified by grace alone is the man who has left all to follow Christ." It's no wonder Paul exclaimed, *"God forbid that I should boast except in the cross of our Lord Jesus Christ"* (Galatians 6:14). We no longer need to strive to be, to do, we are justified by faith in Christ. That is the good, restful news. Dr Martyn Lloyd-Jones sums it up beautifully in his book *Spiritual Depression: its Causes and Cures*:

"To make it quite practical I have a very simple test. After I have explained the way of Christ to somebody I say, 'Now, are you ready to say that you are a Christian?' And they hesitate. And then I say, 'What's the matter? Why are you hesitating?' And so often people say, 'I don't feel like I'm good enough yet. I don't think I'm ready to say I'm a Christian now.' And at once I know that I have been wasting my breath. They are still thinking in terms of themselves ... It sounds very modest to say, 'Well, I don't think I'm good enough,' but it's a very denial of the faith. The very essence of the Christian faith is to say that He is good enough and I am in Him. As long as you go on thinking about yourself like that and saying, 'I'm not good enough; oh, I'm not good enough,' you are denying God – you are denying the gospel ... How can I put it plainly? It doesn't matter if you have almost entered into the depths of hell ... It does not matter from the standpoint of being justified before God at all. You are no more hopeless than the most moral and respectable person in the world."

The walk of justification by faith is a life of surrender, intimacy and longed-for rest. We take on His easy yoke and gently synchronise with his unforced rhythms of grace. *"Keep company with me,"* says Jesus, *"and you'll learn to live freely and lightly."* (Matthew 11:30 MSG)

DAY 50
THE BATTLEFIELD OF THE MIND

"For though we walk in the flesh, we do not war according to the flesh. For the weapons of our warfare are not carnal but mighty in God for pulling down strongholds, casting down arguments and every high thing that exalts itself against the knowledge of God, bringing every thought into captivity to the obedience of Christ."

(2 Corinthians 10:3-5)

We are all in a spiritual battle and the battlefield is our minds. Our thoughts will meander constantly through life, encompassing difficult memories from the past, fears about the future, the opinions of others, messages from the media, the Church and much more. Our enemy's strategy has not altered since he tempted Jesus in the wilderness – he tries to invade our thoughts and persuade us to doubt God's word. He has no authority in our lives except that which we give him through our agreement.

The enemy is constantly looking for ways to deceive, so that he can steal, kill and destroy (John 10:10). He attempts to gain a foothold in our lives (Ephesians 4:27) so that he can establish a stronghold (2 Corinthians 10:3-5) – a belief or attitude that is contrary to God's word and results in behaviour contrary to His will. It begins with the whisper of uncertainty of Eden, "Did God really say...?" or the undermining talk of the wilderness, "If you are a son...".

Now for the good news. We can defeat the machinations of the kingdom of darkness with spiritual weapons. Ephesians 6 speaks about our spiritual armour. For now, let's think about just two pieces. We fight armed with the sword of the Spirit, the Word of God, and defend ourselves with the shield of faith. The latter refers to the resolute making up of our minds to trust in God – who He says He is for us, and what He promises to do for us. We take each thought captive and demolish the arguments that contradict God's word. As Smith Wigglesworth put it "God said it, I believe it, that settles it."

As Steve Backlund has said, "What we believe is ultimately more important than what we do. The course of our lives is set by our deepest core beliefs. These mind-sets are either a stronghold for God's purposes or a playhouse for the enemy of our souls."

The more we align ourselves with what God says, the less we will be powerless, tossed about by every wind of doctrine. In the wilderness, Jesus countered every attack of the enemy with, "It is written....".

Pause to reflect: what do you believe about God? What do you believe God thinks about you? What mind-sets govern your day to day living?

We are transformed as our minds are renewed by the truth of God's word. Ask Father God to uncover any ungodly beliefs that you hold and replace them with His truth. The truth will instantly begin to set you free. Fix your eyes on Jesus, abide in His word, and declare out loud the truth. The kingdom of God will crash in around you!

DAY 51
RAW FAITH

——٠——

What language do you speak? Where is your conversation most at home? E.W. Kenyon said, "Faith talks in the language of God. Doubt talks in the language of man."

Faith is about trusting that God is who He says He is for us, and will do what He has promised. F.F. Bosworth wrote that, "We cannot pray with faith including the faith-destroying phrase 'If it be thy will'." It's a cop out, an options open kind of prayer. James wrote that if we are not in faith we are in doubt (James 1:6), and Paul that whatever is not from faith is sin (Romans 14:27). The author of Hebrews wrote that it is impossible to please God apart from faith (Hebrews 11:6).

Our prayers are ineffective when we are unsure, or doubt the will of God. How do we know His will? We become familiar with God's heart and His will by reading and hearing the word of God and by spending time in His glorious, loving presence. His word sanctifies us (John 17:17), washes us (Ephesians 5:26), renews our mind and aligns it with the will of God (Romans 12:1-2). Faith comes by hearing the word of God (Romans 10:17).

A grace-fuelled confidence is another word for faith. John writes,

"Now this is the confidence that we have in Him, that if we ask anything according to His will, He hears us. And if we know that He hears us, whatever we ask, we know that we have the petitions that we have asked of Him." (1 John 5:14-15)

Martin Luther puts it another way: "Prayer is not overcoming God's reluctance, but laying hold of His willingness."

Often we doubt because we don't feel *full* of faith. But Smith

Wigglesworth exhorts, "I can't understand God by feelings. I can't understand the Lord Jesus Christ by feelings. I can only understand God the Father and Jesus Christ by what the word says about them. God is everything the word says He is. We need to get acquainted with Him through the word."

Get into God's word, be awakened unto His willingness – that's the gift of faith that will move mountains.

DAY 52
TRUE GREATNESS

——•——

"In the company of Jesus there are no experts only
beginners."
–Eugene Peterson

Everyone is born to be great. That might sound like an
overblown claim, but it depends on how one defines greatness.
Every person is significant to God and can become successful
in life, or "great", because greatness is not a destination we
arrive at, but rather a heart posture.

I believe the desire to be great is God-given. It comes
from our great God, in whose image we are made. When the
disciples of Jesus were rather questionably arguing about
who was the greatest among them, He didn't rebuke them
for their desire to be great. Instead He made them question
and re-imagine what true greatness looks like.

*"Jesus intervened: 'Kings like to throw their weight around
and people in authority like to give themselves fancy titles. It's
not going to be that way with you. Let the senior among you
become the junior; let the leader act the part of the servant.
Who would you rather be: the one who eats the dinner or the
one who serves the dinner? You'd rather eat and be served,
right? But I've taken my place among you as one who serves.'"*
(Luke 22:24-30 MSG)

God came to earth as a servant. True greatness is found in
servant-heartedness.

Not only did Jesus take the role of a servant, but He *"made
Himself of no reputation ... coming in the likeness of men"*
(Philippians 2:7). Imagine: the Almighty Creator hid His
divinity is fragile human form, in the person of Christ – an act

of meekness we will never fully understand or appreciate.

When Jesus rebuked the Pharisees, one of His major complaints was that all their works were done "to be seen by men". They loved their impressive titles and marketplace accolades; to be admired as the wisest teachers. Their lives were all about reputation (Matthew 23:5-12).

On the night of His betrayal, Jesus showed us perhaps most famously (John 13) that those who truly know who they are, where they are from, and where they are going, are unconcerned with image and prefer simply to serve. They will even wash the feet of their betrayers. Great people serve and their unglamorous service becomes fragrant worship to God.

Great people have no interest in the limelight because their desire is to glorify Jesus. Great people are humble, teachable, and have a wide-eyed, childlike innocence. When Jesus' disciples asked Him who was the greatest in the kingdom He called over a child and sat him or her on His knee. It was a powerful image. Children were largely ignored by society, considered unimportant. Jesus' phrase, "little children" served to represent all those people considered unimportant, but who reached out to God in humility. Treating the least with care and respect makes us truly great (Matthew 18:5). We will never graduate beyond childlike humility.

"And now abide faith, hope and love, these three; but the greatest of these is love." (1 Corinthians 13:13)

Finally, great people never turn their love off. The greatest men and women on earth are cheerful, often hidden, servants who never graduate beyond beginning. They go low, stopping to love the one in front of them.

Declare our loud with me today: "I'm here to serve, I'm here to learn, I'm here to love. I'm becoming great."

DAY 53
LOVE OVERCOMES

"And so faith, hope, love abide [faith—conviction and belief respecting man's relation to God and divine things; hope—joyful and confident expectation of eternal salvation; love—true affection for God and man, growing out of God's love for and in us], these three; but the greatest of these is love."
— St. Paul

For the remaining 8 days of this book we will meditate on love. Love is a choice; the "greatest" choice. Love is grace, as Christ, the embodiment of love, lives in and loves through us. Love is an act of the will, not a feeling. As we study love, all of these love-traits inform us of God's immutable character.

Love Shines

"And you, who once were alienated and enemies in your mind by wicked works..." (Colossians 1:21). Who are the people God wants to love through you and me? It is those who are alienated from Him in their hearts and minds. Remember that God didn't wait for us to change before He loved us – He shone His light into our darkness. Find those who seem the furthest from God and let your love shine.

Love is Thankful

What a miserable state of being is that of entitlement. When we are poor in thankfulness we are rich in covetousness, entitlement and estrangement from God. Thanksgiving, however, is heaven's red carpet. Thanksgiving is a key to intimacy. Thanksgiving is an expression of trust in God's ability. We are to trust Him at all times and in everything give thanks – these truths are inseparable.

Love Casts out Fear

We are built for connection and intimacy with God and man. Martin Copenhaver writes, "Everyone has a basic human need to be seen, that is, to be understood and valued. You can't fake truly seeing another person. People know if you really see them or not. When you truly see them, you find their note, their vibration, their connection with God, and you dance with them right there."

When we live in fear we build walls to try to protect ourselves. Shame, reinforced by fear, ensures we won't let anyone truly see us or truly know us. We live a disabled version of ourselves. If we have not been perfected in love then we function more like a broken cistern than a child of God. We cannot give what we don't have! We must dare to embrace God's love for us fully – allow His healing light into every dark place. His perfect love working in us and through us dispels all fear.

Love Acts

Smith Wigglesworth said that the Book of Acts was written because the apostles acted. As Heidi Baker says, "Love looks like something." Love is compelled to act; to obey Jesus' command to "go". People are drowning in the sea of indecision. We need to wade in and pull them out, not sit idly on the beach! Let's ask God to set us on fire with His purposes and help us to win souls – whatever that looks like for each one of us.

DAY 54
LOVE NEVER RUNS OUT

Love is Faithful

You could say that in his lifetime Isaiah was a failure because nobody listened to him – the people's hearts just got harder and harder. We are reminded of Jesus' words:

"There's trouble ahead when you live only for the approval of others, saying what flatters them, doing what indulges them. Popularity contests are not truth contests—look how many scoundrel preachers were approved by your ancestors! Your task is to be true, not popular." (Luke 6:26 MSG)

History reveals that our success lies in our faithfulness to God, nothing else, so be encouraged! Isaiah was a truth teller, fearless in his delivery because he had seen God's glory and heard His voice. Freely we have received, freely we now give. All for love.

Love is Inefficient

Sometimes love looks like a waste of time, money or talent. It appears to many to be inefficient, at least on the surface. The truth is, loving people well is sacrificial, inconvenient and costs us. It goes against the grain of our task-orientated, super-efficient western culture. Mary "wasted" a whole year's salary on Jesus in an act of worship. The disciples missed the point and moaned about her use of money. Jesus let them know that this sacrificial act would be remembered wherever the gospel was preached for centuries to come. Kingdom love turns the world upside down.

Love is Patient

Love is patient. Patience is large and generous. Love lives in the abundance of cheerful, perpetual giving, without rights, without guarantees, without accolades. Impatience is lean, small and selfish. The largeness of love overlooks the current state of people's lives to see them at the end of their race. It calls out the "gold" in them that they are oblivious to. Patient love honours someone for who they are, without stumbling over who they are not. There is spacious grace in love.

Love Suffers Long

God's love is potting soil for kindness and mercy. Love never seeks its own, so is no man's debtor. Love doesn't look for a return. The patient lover lacks nothing. We are saved to be love, more than we are to need love.

DAY 55
LOVE DESIRES HIS PRESENCE

———·———

Love is Holy

God is holy. The Church is called to be holy. To be holy means "to be set apart". It doesn't meant "to fit in" or "to be relevant". We are only relevant *when* we are holy. Made in God's image, holiness is part of our spiritual DNA. Each of us is a pilgrim journeying towards our true identity, a place of rest and belonging. A lack of holiness is what feeds mankind's craving to be popular at the expense of pleasing God. Holy love is a burning torch that leads people out of darkness.

Holiness is a choice – to set ourselves apart for Him alone; to seek Jesus first and follow Him without compromise. Holiness comes as we are ever-filled with His presence. As Graham Cooke put it, the imperative to, *"Be holy as I am holy"* (1 Peter 1:16) is not a cold, religious command, but a loving benediction, spoken by the only One who can make us holy.

Love is Obedient

God chases His beloved and His beloved chase after His love. Love is the opposite of selfishness. Love manifests itself in a life of obedience. Love is responsive to the Father. Love continues to walk with God and is not diverted by people or circumstances. It doesn't fly off the handle, it seeks to understand, listen and learn. Love is not defensive, touchy or fretful because there is no fear in love. Love is never threatened (1 Corinthians 13:5).

Love is Grateful

Love is always grateful. It's not envious and doesn't get jealous, because it's impossible to be like that when we are genuinely grateful. Love looks for the blessing of God everywhere and acknowledges it. It always looks for the best (1 Corinthians 13:4).

Love is Humble

Love is humble. Love has a realistic understanding of self. Love doesn't need to play God. Love is not entitled, insisting on its own rights. Love is not vainglorious or conceited. Love doesn't need to win an argument, because it is not proud. Love is humble, releasing others and preferring to lift them up. Love never gets offended (1 Corinthians 13:4-5).

DAY 56
LOVE NEVER FAILS

Love Accepts

Love accepts and loves myself and others as they are. Nobody is unacceptable. Acceptance is the beginning of healing. Self-rejection, and the rejection of others, hosts brokenness. Self-acceptance is acceptance of self in spite of weaknesses or deficiencies. Soren Kierkegaard wrote, "The most common form of despair is not being who you are. To be that self which one truly is, is indeed the opposite of despair."

"God demonstrates His own love toward us, in that while we were still sinners, Christ died for us." (Romans 5:8)

The Lord models accepting love. Can we really say that we are emotionally healthy until we can love others where they are at, just as they are? We are powerless to change others anyway – only God can do that – so we'd better just love them! It's God's job to change a person's heart. We can choose to love them unconditionally and sow truths into their lives, led by the Spirit, that will help them on their journey.

Love first accepts. That acceptance is the first step on the journey towards salvation.

Love is Secure

Love is completely secure and sure of itself. It doesn't need to be right in an effort to disguise its shame. Love doesn't need to be liked by everyone, nor understood. There is no defensiveness in love.

Love Empowers

Love empowers others to become what God has made them

to be. Love values where someone is at (1 Corinthians 13:7), for God doesn't judge us for where we are on our journey, but for whom we refuse to become.

Love Wonders

Love wonders. Love dreams. Love is childlike. G.K. Chesterton wrote, "We are perishing for want of wonder, not for want of wonders." (1 Corinthians 13:7)

DAY 57
LOVE LAUGHS BUT ALSO FIGHTS

Love is Light-Hearted

Love laughs. Children laugh easily. Unbelief and self-sufficiency result in anxiety and heaviness. Psalm 2:4 says that "He who sits in the heavens shall laugh." Why? Because He reigns. Laughter shares the perspective of our Sovereign Abba – the overcoming, victorious perspective of the cross and resurrection. Religious striving in all its forms is grim faced, while love laughs and rejoices in the supernatural victory of the cross where all striving ceased.

Laughter is a sign that we have grasped the enormity of the good news. Religious people don't laugh much and get offended when the childlike laugh, dance and shout. Children of God inherit freely by grace, with great joy.

Love is restful, trusting, relaxed, fun. Love doesn't take itself or anything too seriously because love humbly trusts that God reigns and God is good. Karl Barth wrote that "Laughter is the closest thing to the grace of God."

Watch children play. They like having fun and can do so because they are free of the responsibility to run their own lives. The kingdom belongs to such as these. When we are too busy to laugh, dance and enjoy life, it is often because we have taken back control.

Laughter is the key to finding the heart of God. God laughs a lot and likes having fun. He created both and wants none of us to miss out on His creation.

Love is the Highest Form of Spiritual Warfare

Love never fails. Physical touch, words of affirmation, acts

of service, spending quality time with others, giving gifts —
these five love languages disarm and cast out the darkness.
Love destroys fear. The most powerful, pleasing to God, devil-
terrifying thing you can do today is to be loved by the Father,
love Him in return, love yourself well and then love others
in the same manner (1 Corinthians 13:8, Matthew 22:37-39).

Love is Respectful to All

Love is respectful. It honours every person and their free
will. Love refuses to manipulate or control. Love chooses
connection, builds up, and encourages (1 Corinthians 13:5).
Thomas Merton wrote, "The beginning of love is to let those
we love be perfectly themselves, and not to twist them to fit
our own image."

DAY 58
LOVE NEVER ENDS

Love is Powerful
Love is powerful and self-controlled. Love flows from the inside out, like a gushing river that can't be stopped.

Love is Selfless
Love is not selfish or self-conscious. Love is God-conscious. Love is not narcissistic. Love doesn't force itself on others and doesn't self-promote. Love is happy to be last and puts others first (1 Corinthians 13:5).

Love is Timeless and Unchanging
I like how Shakespeare speaks of love in his famous sonnet: "Love is not love which alters when it alteration finds ... it is an ever-fixed mark, that looks on tempests, and is never shaken...". God is love. His love, His word will never change.

Love is Peaceful
To be full of God's love is to know real peace. Peace comes when we allow God to take an axe to the roots of our independence.

Love is Courageous
Love is courageous. Courage is not the absence of fear but the mastery of it. Courage denies fear in the face of a greater love. Courage obeys and worships God, whatever the cost.

DAY 59
LOVE IS TRUE

Love Rejoices in the Truth

Love rejoices in the truth (1 Corinthians 13:6). Truth appears 118 times in the New Testament. Truth is actually an eternal Person (John 14:6) who cannot change. Truth is love and grace because both are Jesus (1 John 4:16, John 10:30, John 1:14).

Truth is not relative or changing. Love is true, not fashionable. Love rejoices and proclaims truth and righteousness.

Love is not cowardly and selfish, it is courageous and sacrificial. Love puts on courage and finds a rooftop in order to proclaim the truth! Truth presented without love is harsh and cutting. It pushes people into being defensive. But love given without truth is dishonest. It leads people to believe that things are OK when they aren't.

Love Believes the Best

Love is always ready to believe the best of every person (1 Corinthians 13:7). Love refuses to step into unholy judgement and comparison. Comparison will either make you feel superior or inferior to your neighbour and is rooted in pride and fertilised by shame. Cling to Jesus for dear life!

Love Never Fails

Your fear of failure will be dealt the deadliest of blows if you believe the Scripture and simply keep your love on! Simply abide in the Vine, receive from Him, then live from the overflow. To the degree that you gaze at His face, to that degree your face will release His gaze – His love. Love always wins.

DAY 60
LOVE RISES ABOVE EVERYTHING

Love is a Fire

The scripture says "Our God is a consuming fire" (Hebrews 12:29). Love is a fire. As our nations are wracked with secularism and Luke-warmness, we should burn with the fire of God. May God shake everything that is man-made and get us lying face down once again, utterly dependent on His supernatural power!

Love Rests

Restless people have to stay busy. To stop and just "be" is counterintuitive to most – even painful, because it means confronting those aspects of our lives we'd prefer to gloss over. People will always try to escape their inner poverty with outward activity. But if we are restless, we are probably rootless and spiritually shallow. Joy and peace come from a heart that has been stilled before God, filled with the presence of the Holy Spirit, and is in communion with Jesus.

True rest, peace and joy will leave you content in all circumstances, because you are truly rich on the inside. This is mine and your inheritance in Christ. We must cease to be slaves to the idolatry of distraction, materialism and busyness, and just be still and know that He is God. Amen!

ABOUT THE AUTHOR

DOMINIC MUIR leads Nowbelieve Ministries, which he founded in 2005 and is a grass roots, counter-cultural community of believers with a strong desire to live and share an authentic expression of the Gospel. Proclaiming the message of good news publicly has been a key feature of the ministry, which has seen many saved and healed.

Dom had a career as a film-maker and marketeer before having a powerful encounter with the Holy Spirit and surrendering his life to Jesus. He served as an intern at Holy Trinity Brompton before being called into full time ministry.

Dom is married to Thea and they travel internationally, preaching, teaching and sharing the love and grace of God. For information and updates see: https://www.facebook.com/HungryDom/

28282713R00090

Printed in Poland
by Amazon Fulfillment
Poland Sp. z o.o., Wrocław